DUNGEONS

&

DRAWINGS

An Illustrated Compendium of Creatures

Blanca Martínez de Rituerto & Joe Sparrow

Andrews McMeel
PUBLISHING®

Andrews McMeel Publishing
a division of Andrews McMeel Universal
1130 Walnut Street, Kansas City, Missouri 64106

www.andrewsmcmeel.com

22 23 24 25 26 RLP 10 9 8 7 6 5 4 3

ISBN: 978-1-5248-5201-6

Library of Congress Control Number: 2019938984

Editor: Katie Gould
Designer: Sierra S. Stanton
Production Editor: Margaret Daniels
Production Manager: Chuck Harper

ATTENTION: SCHOOLS AND BUSINESSES

Andrews McMeel books are available at quantity discounts with bulk purchase for educational, business, or sales promotional use. For information, please e-mail the Andrews McMeel Publishing Special Sales Department:
specialsales@amuniversal.com.

Table of Contents

Introduction

My first experience actually playing a fantasy tabletop role-playing game was when I was around ten years old. I'll spare you the details of my character, except to say he was a hybrid of warrior and wizard (a new concept that I found unspeakably cool) and wielded a bastard sword (mostly picked for the transgressive thrill of saying its name). The campaign was short-lived—we fought some orcs and some kind of small dragon, I think—but one memory that really sticks in my head was being permitted by our Dungeon Master to peruse the so-called "Monster Manual," one of several books in which the game's labyrinthine rules were supposedly contained.

It's safe to say that my ten-year-old mind was completely blown. This document—shiny and hardback, but decorated as if it were a leathery old tome—not only contained illustrations and descriptions for the four or five creatures we had faced, but dozens of others as well. It induced in me a sort of narrative vertigo—making it starkly clear that the portion of the game world that we (a party of perhaps level 1 or 2) had experienced was but one tiny part of a cosmos of creatures that spanned whole dimensions. I had thought the Skeleton Lord we just fought (and barely defeated) was a worthy foe; now I was reading about beasts the size of houses, fiends that could petrify with a glance, tentacled horrors that would devour their prey mind, body, and soul. It was both humbling and terribly exciting. I, of course, immediately enquired of our DM what the "strongest monster" was, expecting something familiar to me like a dragon or a lich. Instead, he turned to a page bearing the name "Tarasque" and an illustration of a fearsome, Godzilla-like monster. It was awesome. The image stuck in my head.

We pronounced it "Tara-skew" at the time, because we didn't know the name was actually French (it's pronounced "Ta-rask"). We didn't know that it came from an old folktale of a shelled dragon that supposedly terrorized the south of France in the first millennium, or that it was driven off by a saint called Martha. We didn't know that there's still a town named after it—Tarascon—either. There are theories that it might have been some sort of hippo or a large tortoise.

More often than not, behind even the most fantastical beast lurks the specter of a truth. Monsters rarely pop into existence out of nowhere, and in many cases—such as in the Tarasque's —the longer they linger, the more mythology they accrue. What started out as a tortoise scaring peasants in medieval France gradually turned into a colossal, civilization-threatening monster (with a one-in-six chance to reflect any spell or projectile back at its user!). Folklore is a vibrant patchwork, constantly being added to and taken away from—and that process is very much ongoing in the work of fantasy authors, RPG writers, and imaginative GMs everywhere.

Obviously as artists, our main thrill is in coming up with cool and imaginative ways to depict these creatures. But it's our interest in that patchwork of folklore and history (and the two are often inseparable) that keeps us coming back to this subject and ultimately drove us to make this book. *Dungeons & Drawings* actually started as an art blog way back in 2010 when Blanca and I were fresh out of art school. Our time studying had, for both of us, reignited our interest in tabletop RPGs and fantasy, and we were both avidly writing new stories and campaigns of our own. We would post illustrations every week or as often as we could manage, in an attempt to fill our time between paid jobs (which were admittedly a little thin on the ground at the time).

What started as an exercise became a passion, and that passion quickly attracted followers from all over the world as we uploaded new illustrations. Now, with this book, we've compiled the definitive collection of more than 100 of our favorite illustrations from across the last nine years, as well as over twenty brand-new creature designs that have never seen the light of day anywhere. Each monster is accompanied not only by a flavorful description and some easy-to-understand stats, but also a well-researched look at its folkloric origins in real world history. You might be surprised at what you discover about certain classic beasts—we certainly were on many occasions! Did you know, for example, that angels were once commonly depicted as quadrupedal, sphinxlike beings? Or that the word "kobold" shares its origin with the chemical element cobalt?

Anyway—I've probably rambled enough for this introduction, so let me just wrap up with a genuine, heartfelt thanks from both Blanca and myself to absolutely everyone who has followed our work on this project over the last decade. The engagement and encouragement we've had from friends and strangers alike has been so heartening, and it has pushed both of us to progress further as artists than I think we ever would have on our own. This book represents a lot of time and hard work from both of us, and we're very proud to be able to share it with you.

Stay monstrous!
Joe Sparrow
2018

Key

This section explains the various symbols used to categorize each creature, as well as the scoring system used to indicate the strength of their abilities.

Alignment

Alignment is the moral disposition that each creature has. This is a good measure of their compassion or sense of altruism—a good-aligned being is much more likely to be trustworthy or make decisions that help the adventurer. Most creatures of animallike intelligence are considered incapable of the philosophizing necessary to make moral considerations and are as such categorized as neutral.

Note that a good alignment does not necessarily mean a creature is nonviolent or poses no threat to the adventurer. Creatures possessing certain magical abilities or inherent charisma may be able to mask their alignment or sometimes pose as another.

Good

These creatures are moved by benevolence and altruism, generally striving to help the weak and needy. While they are sometimes naïve and can be manipulated or tricked, the more experienced among them know to temper kindness with wariness.

Neutral

These creatures are neither good nor evil. With animals and the mindless, this is simply the inability to understand morality. Among sentient beings, it can imply a disregard for the consequences of one's actions, whether good or ill.

Evil

These creatures are driven by self-interest and sadism. Lacking empathy, they are comfortable using any means, including deceit, to achieve their goals. Indeed, they may enjoy offering the facade of friendship only to later betray a companion.

Element

The classical **elements** are the building blocks of life, reflecting temperament, strengths, physical makeup, supernatural abilities, and home environment. All creatures are a mix of these elements, though never in perfect balance; one is always dominant over the rest.

A creature that is strongly aligned with one element may prove weak to its opposite counterpart—with the exception of Void, which has no opposing element.

The sky, light, speed, and sound are associated with this element. Its creatures may be ethereal, capable of flight, or invisible. They can be absentminded and prone to flights of fancy.

Air

Willfulness, anger, passion, destruction, and creation are associated with this element. Its creatures may be impulsive or dangerous, though not necessarily evil.

Fire

Nothingness, eternity, the immaterial, and abstraction are associated with this element. Its creatures may seem inscrutable or strange, as if driven by forces outside of human experience.

Void

Emotion, cold, mystery, and mutability are associated with this element. Its creatures often live underwater. They are likely curious, fickle, and unreliable.

Water

Nature, stability, minerals, and flesh are associated with this element. Its creatures may be stoic or dull, but they are highly durable and resistant to change.

Earth

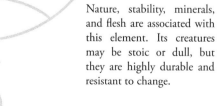

Type

Just as the animal kingdom can be broken into phylum, class, and species, it is possible to divide supernatural creatures into certain **types**. These categories not only take into account the physical form of the creature, but also its spiritual characteristics, origins, inherent nature, and level of magical ability. Some creatures may exhibit characteristics of more than one type, in which case they have generally been placed into the category that suits them best for the sake of clarity.

Beast

Animalistic creatures that have little in the way of humanoid features, if any. Magical beasts may look like combinations of several mundane animals, the results ranging from horror to majesty. This category has no bearing on the intelligence of the creature —some beasts are of an intelligence beyond human and are in fact responsible for teaching or leading humanoid races.

Examples: Cockatrice, Dragon, Sphinx

Construct

Creatures that have been built from non-living parts and animated using alchemy or magic. Most are simple automatons, only capable of following orders. More complex constructs may have spirits trapped inside them to animate them or otherwise have a soul, granting them higher intelligence or outright sentience. Truly intelligent constructs are often quite naïve when they first come to life, which can prove dangerous when combined with their above-average strength and durability.

Examples: Colossus, Golem, Homunculus

Humanoid

Creatures having mostly humanlike bodies or features. They are usually bipedal, possessing at least two arms and a face. Creatures in this category are sentient, but their intelligence can range from animal dullness to godlike genius.

Examples: Giant, Hag, Werewolf

Fairy

Creatures that embody an aspect of the natural world or are the soul of a place or object given form. Their bodies can be a combination of animal, plant, or humanoid, although they often use illusory magic to alter their appearance. Their wellbeing is attached to that of the land on which they live. Their personalities, too, are a reflection of nature—ranging from nurturing kindness, to predatory cruelty, to fickle indifference. Many fairies prefer to be referred to by deferential titles, such as the Good People or the Hidden Folk.

Examples: Kelpie, Nymph, Satyr

Outsider

Creatures who, in one way or another, are not native to the material plane. They may be the inhabitants of other dimensions such as Heaven, Hell, and the Dreamworld, or else be the physical representations of laws of the Universe. They are otherworldly beings, subsisting primarily on spiritual or cosmic energies, including human souls. Due to their alien nature, outsiders are inherently magical.

Examples: Angel, Demon, Elemental

Plant

Creatures that are made entirely of vegetable or fungal matter. While the majority of plants are non-sentient, static, and feed by absorbing sunlight or nutrients from the earth, magical plants may have animal or humanlike intelligence, be ambulatory, or seek out living prey. All plants in this book are potentially deadly to ordinary mortals.

Examples: Bomb Plant, Mushroomfolk, Treant

Undead

Creatures that continue to move despite biological arrest, existing in either a physical or ethereal form. The state of undeath can be induced by spiritual discontent, dark magic, or spirits taking possession of a body. Sentient undead creatures tend towards evil, generally having a loathing for the living. However, advocates for the use of necromancy will argue that the type as a whole be considered neutral.

Examples: Banshee, Vampire, Zombie

Combat Magic

 A very weak or otherwise poor physical fighter.   Inherently supernatural, but having no active magical abilities.

 Having the combat ability of the average unarmed human.   Basic magical ability, being able to cast a limited number of weak spells.

 Being equipped with lethal weapons (whether natural or manufactured) or otherwise trained in combat.   Possessing a moderate magical aptitude through natural ability or tutelage.

 Can easily take on multiple foes or destroy buildings.   Having superior magical powers or arcane knowledge.

✹ ✹ ✹ ✹ ✹ Having physical strength on par with natural disasters.   Having magical abilities that can warp reality.

Smarts	Loot	Danger
Animallike intelligence.	Items of common or poor make. Flesh may be edible.	A largely harmless creature that would prefer to flee than fight.
Sentient and capable of speech, but with intelligence below that of the average human.	Items of decent make or of semiprecious materials. Body parts can be used in weak magic.	Creatures that will defend themselves when confronted.
Intelligence comparable to that of the average human.	Items of good make, fine materials, or having magical qualities. Body parts can be used in intermediate magic.	Aggressive creatures that may seek out human prey.
Being of genius or otherwise superhuman intelligence.	Massive amounts of riches. Powerful magical items or spell ingredients.	Creatures capable of easily causing permanent crippling injuries or madness.
Inconceivable intelligence.	Unique magical items or enough treasure to last several lifetimes.	Creatures of soul-destroying or apocalyptic threat.

Ahuizotl

a.k.a. Lake Panther,
Nguruvilu

COMBAT	✦ ✦ ✦ ✧ ✧
MAGIC	✦ ✦ ✧ ✧ ✧
SMARTS	✦ ✧ ✧ ✧ ✧
LOOT	✦ ✦ ✧ ✧ ✧
DANGER	✦ ✦ ✦ ✧ ✧

An aquatic beast, as large as a crocodile, that makes its home in murky rivers, lakes, and caverns. It has grasping, humanlike hands and a larger, equally dexterous hand at the end of a prehensile tail. The body is vaguely canine or feline and its back is covered in spines. If you find a body floating in the river, there are several signs to look for to determine whether it was the victim of an ahuizotl. Firstly, the body will be covered in hand-shaped bruises, left over from the beast's strangling attacks. Secondly, the body will be missing a combination of fingernails, teeth, and eyes. Those who manage to escape it say they were drawn to the water's edge by the sound of a weeping child, only to find the ahuizotl waiting for them instead.

Adventurer's Tip: Watch out for unexpected whirlpools, as ahuizotls create these water hazards in an attempt to capsize small water vessels.

The ahuizotl ("spiny water-thing" in Nahuatl) is a creature of Aztec myth. It is associated with Tlaloc, the god of rain and storms, as those who die by drowning are sent to his afterlife. The mishipeshu of Ojibwa and Algonquin legend, also known as the Great Lynx, is a similar creature. This catlike monster is covered in metal spines and attacks humans who swim or row in its lakes. The mishipeshu is said to be in constant conflict with thunderbirds.

Angel

a.k.a. Celestial,
Heavenly Servant

COMBAT	☼	☼	☼	☼	☼
MAGIC	☼	☼	☼	☼	☼
SMARTS	☼	☼	☼	☼	☼
LOOT	☼	☼	☼	☼	☼
DANGER	☼	☼	☼	☼	☼

A servant of the holy deities and bastion of all things good. At different turns messengers, diplomats, and warriors (and uncompromisingly efficient in all three roles), angels strike holy terror into the hearts of evil creatures everywhere with their masterful combat prowess and searing holy light. As an angel's true form is incomprehensible to mortals, they take on a humanoid appearance when visiting an earthly charge. Even this doesn't fully disguise their heavenly qualities, however; they appear beautiful and genderless, have wings, and shed a strange luminous aura that inspires both love and fear. Legends tell of a rebellion in Heaven eons ago, where angels who turned against their masters were cast out and transformed into demons.

Adventurer's Tip: If you are good, be not afraid. If you are evil, be very afraid.

Angels (from the Latin angelus, *meaning "messenger") have their origins in Abrahamic myth. Mentioned on a number of occasions in the Torah, they typically serve by relaying the will of God to humans. Very early images depict them as monstrous, sphinxlike beings similar to the Assyrian shedu, but later Christian interpretations popularize their form as winged, haloed humanoids. Other religions have their own equivalent to these divine servants, such as the Zoroastrian fravashi.*

Archdevil

a.k.a. The Beast,
Demogorgon

COMBAT ☼ ☼ ☼ ☼ ☼
MAGIC ☼ ☼ ☼ ☼ ☼
SMARTS ☼ ☼ ☼ ☼ ☼
LOOT ☼ ☼ ☼ ☼ ☼
DANGER ☼ ☼ ☼ ☼ ☼

The most powerful demons and devils of the infernal planes, sitting at the top of a strict class system where the weak are food for the strong. A terrifying combination of intellect, magic, physical strength, and ruthlessness, archdevils are to be feared perhaps above all other creatures. They are often too busy managing wars between the hellish factions and against the celestial hosts to concern themselves overmuch with mortal affairs, letting lesser fiends act as their proxies. Summoning an archdevil is both extremely difficult and extremely hazardous, both to the summoner and to the ground it is summoned on—locations have been known to be permanently cursed by the brief appearance of these infernal kings.

Adventurer's Tip: Pacts with archdevils are seldom worth it. Even if you best them, you may be barred from afterlives both good and evil.

Almost all hells across various religions have especially powerful demons who rule over their lesser brethren. While the most famous archdevil in the Abrahamic religions is the fallen angel Satan, The Lesser Key of Solomon, a seventeenth century grimoire, lists seventy-two other similarly powerful fiends. Each has their own aristocratic title, magic sigil, armies, and specialist knowledge that they pass on to those who summon them.

Bacchae

a.k.a. Maenads

COMBAT	☀	☀	☀	☼	☼
MAGIC	☀	☀	☼	☼	☼
SMARTS	☀	☀	☼	☼	☼
LOOT	☀	☀	☼	☼	☼
DANGER	☀	☼	☼	☼	☼

A group of joyful spirits who tear through the countryside on a never-ending party, wearing animal skins and vine leaves, if anything at all. The arrival of the bacchae is heralded by the clashing din of drums, pipes, and cymbals from beyond the hills. Anything they strike starts weeping milk, honey, or liquor. As a physical embodiment of drunkenness, they possess brutal strength, confidence, and impulsiveness, and little to no empathy or foresight. Their madness swings between joy and rage, and any unfortunate who crosses their path will either be torn to shreds and eaten, or forced to join in their revelry. Mortal participants don't share their hosts' magical immunities, and will often be found in the following days naked and dead from exhaustion.

Adventurer's Tip: If you hear their music, run. Locked doors will not stop them.

The bacchae are the female members of the entourage of Bacchus, the Roman god of wine and madness. The first bacchae were actually the god's victims, mortals driven mad when they refused to worship him. The Bacchanalia are a set of Roman festivals dedicated to Bacchus and marked by extreme violence, sexuality, and drunkenness. Among their rituals is the killing of a sacrificial bull with their bare hands.

Bad Clown

a.k.a. The Crooked Man,
The Pied Piper

COMBAT	☀	☀	☼	☼	☼	
MAGIC	☀	☀	☀	☼	☼	
SMARTS	☀	☀	☀	☼	☼	
LOOT	☀	☀	☀	☼	☼	
DANGER	☀	☀	☀	☀	☼	

An emotion-devouring monster hidden under silly ruffles and makeup, its true form known only to its victims. Even in disguise, the proportions of the bad clown are wrong, more extreme and grotesque than any ordinary jester. The makeup doesn't wipe off, its clothes don't get dirty or torn, regardless of tumbling or japes, and its colors are simultaneously washed out and impossibly vibrant. Children are the favorite prey of the bad clown, who are easily led away by its songs and shenanigans. Those taken away by the clown are seldom seen again, though some of its victims have been found in strange isolated places. These unfortunate escapees seem to have the joy and color drained out of them and remain in a catatonic state until the clown comes back for them.

Adventurer's Tip: Beware of carnivals and circuses that appear overnight and disappear just as quickly.

The subversion of the clown as malevolent being began as early as the sixteenth century, with Italy's Pulcinella (Mr. Punch in the English-speaking world). Able to mock his betters with few consequences, the court fool could be interpreted as an agent of chaos. The fear of clowns is called coulrophobia and is inspired by the unnatural appearance and behavior of the entertainers. Some people may feel a similar fear towards mimes, puppets, and other such grotesqueries. These fears have led to a number of genre films and TV shows.

Bajang

a.k.a. Jungle Imp

COMBAT	☀ ☀ ☼ ☼ ☼
MAGIC	☀ ☀ ☀ ☼ ☼
SMARTS	☀ ☀ ☀ ☼ ☼
LOOT	☀ ☀ ☀ ☼ ☼
DANGER	☀ ☀ ☀ ☼ ☼

A jungle spirit that can take on the form of a civet and is often enslaved by warlocks to act as a familiar by trapping it in the body of a stillborn boy-child. While imprisoned in this way, the bajang performs evil tasks for its master, primarily tormenting his enemies with hallucinations and seizures. When not in use, the bajang should be kept in a box, and regularly fed on eggs and blood. If the spirit is not properly fed, it can rebel against its master, killing him and running amok as it searches for sustenance. Wild bajangs love to eat children—the younger the better—and even pregnant women have awoken to find claw marks on their bellies from a bajang's attempt to tear out their unborn child.

Adventurer's Tip: Spirit slaves made with a children's corpse aren't reliable; they are prone to childish impulses and are easily distracted from their mission by toys or candy.

The bajang is one of several Malaysian spirits or demons that spontaneously form or can be created from the body parts of stillborns. Other creatures include the pelesit (a cricket-spirit made from the tongue of a dead first-born), the toyol (from a fetus), and the pontianak (from a female stillborn). Bajangs and pelesit familiars can be ancient, as a well-cared for familiar will be passed down through the family like some kind of gruesome heirloom.

Baku

a.k.a. Dream-Eater

COMBAT	☼ ☼ ☼ ☼ ☼	
MAGIC	☼ ☼ ☼ ☼ ☼	
SMARTS	☼ ☼ ☼ ☼ ☼	
LOOT	☼ ☼ ☼ ☼ ☼	
DANGER	☼ ☼ ☼ ☼ ☼	

A predatory beast that sports powerful claws and tusks and exists primarily in the Dreamworld. Despite their natural weapons, the baku can't harm corporeal things and only feeds on dreamstuff. A person's awakening can disrupt a baku's feeding, resulting in the telltale fragmentary recollection of one's dreams. These animals can be summoned to consume nightmares, but this should be done sparingly, as the baku is a very greedy beast. Once all the bad dreams have been eaten, they may move on to pleasant dreams, wishes, and hopes, dealing permanent damage to the sleeper's psyche. Blankets made from their pelts offer protection from nightmares and can also ward against evil spirits and disease.

Adventurer's Tip: Over-hunting of baku means that they're now reluctant to come near adult sleepers; they would rather safely feed on the dreams of children.

> *The baku as it's known today is a popular Japanese chimera, though it was originally the mò, a beast of Chinese folklore. Amulets, statues, and pillows in the baku's shape supposedly protect from bad dreams. Older images of the baku show it as a combination of elephant, tiger, and ox, but modern illustrations often depict it as a tapir, a real piglike animal with a short trunk. Despite its appearance, the tapir's closest living relatives are rhinoceroses and horses. The Japenese term for tapir is* baku.

Banshee

a.k.a. Wailing Woman

COMBAT ☆ ☆ ☆ ☆ ☆
MAGIC ✸ ✸ ✸ ☆ ☆
SMARTS ✸ ✸ ☆ ☆ ☆
LOOT ✸ ☆ ☆ ☆ ☆
DANGER ✸ ✸ ☆ ☆ ☆

A vengeful ghost, born from the death of a woman who was either murdered or driven to suicide. This raging spirit relentlessly haunts the person she perceives as the cause of her death, following them to the ends of the earth. She wails and screams, never allowing her victim a moment's peace until they are either driven mad, die from guilt and fear, or kill themselves. Even death doesn't mark the end of the banshee's curse, as she'll move on to her victim's relatives. Her torment will continue until the bloodline is completely destroyed, and after that she haunts the family home for centuries, killing anyone who dares enter it. The older a banshee is, the stronger her scream becomes, so that even hearing it causes instant death.

Adventurer's Tip: The banshee can't be appeased. Only an exorcism will end her haunting.

From the Irish bean sidhe *("female spirit"), although many Celtic cultures have their own name for these ominous women. Though modern banshees are most often depicted as vengeful ghosts, older folklore sometimes depicts them as fairy women whose cries predict the passing of great members of significant Irish families. The Japanese* onryo *("vengeful ghost") can be male or female, but the sinister croaking that precedes her attacks makes Kayako of the* Ju-On *film series similar to a banshee.*

Basilisk

*a.k.a. King of Snakes,
Regulus, Sibilus*

COMBAT	☀ ☀ ○ ○ ○
MAGIC	☀ ☀ ☀ ○ ○
SMARTS	☀ ○ ○ ○ ○
LOOT	☀ ☀ ☀ ○ ○
DANGER	☀ ☀ ☀ ○ ○

A creature born from a snake's egg hatched by a rooster. The basilisk is a serpentlike creature that scurries along on many tiny, almost vestigial, legs. The scales on its head are especially shiny, hardening into crownlike growths as the creature matures. Its gaze and hiss cause blindness and paralysis and can petrify the victim if the basilisk is fully grown. Even when slain, the basilisk is dangerous, as its blood is so toxic that it'll ooze up the weapon that killed it, poisoning the wielder. If a place that was plentiful in snakes is suddenly devoid of them, it's a sure sign that a basilisk is about, as common serpents fear it. The basilisk also inspires a strong loathing and aggression in weasels and mongooses, animals expert in the killing of snakes and immune to the monster's deadly gaze.

Adventurer's Tip: Burn the body of a basilisk to neutralize its poison. After that, the ashes can be safely collected for use in alchemy.

> *The name basilisk comes from the Greek* basilikos, *meaning "little king," referring to its dominion over snakes and the crownlike markings on its head. This creature may be inspired by the cobra, a very venomous subtropical snake with a patterned hood (i.e. the basilisk's crown). Some snakes can squirt their venom a short distance, possibly accounting for the basilisk's deadly "gaze." The cockatrice is a creature related to the basilisk, to the point that older texts use them interchangeably.*

Bhut

a.k.a. Onryo,
Vengeful Ghost

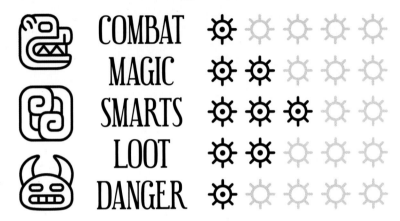

COMBAT ☀ ☆ ☆ ☆ ☆
MAGIC ☀ ☀ ☆ ☆ ☆
SMARTS ☀ ☀ ☀ ☆ ☆
LOOT ☀ ☀ ☆ ☆ ☆
DANGER ☀ ☆ ☆ ☆ ☆

The restless spirit of a person who died both violently and prematurely. Unless given proper funerary rites, the bhut will stay on this earthly plane until the end of what should have been its natural life. The ghost's fury at its early death leads to an all-consuming loathing of the living; they haunt the location where they died, trying to trick passersby into meeting the same fate that they did. Bhuts try to keep their human form, but they cannot seem to get it completely right; there's always some twisted limb or unnatural color about them. Their separation from the mortal realm is further marked by their inability to touch the ground, instead floating a few inches above it, and the distant nasal whine of their voices.

Adventurer's Tip: Bhuts, like many other types of ghost, can be repelled by strong smells, with the scent of burning spices being especially offensive to them.

> Bhut *is the generic term for "ghost" in Hindi. Though generally the ghost of someone who died a premature death, sometimes the term can be applied to a number of spirits, either undead or demonic. In this varied definition, the bhut can be vampiric or harmless, as tall as a giant (if the deceased led an especially sinful and violent life) or the size of a thumb (if they died as a infant or were stillborn).*

Black Squirrel

a.k.a. Light-Eater

COMBAT ☼ ☼ ☼ ☼ ☼

MAGIC ☼ ☼ ☼ ☼ ☼

SMARTS ☼ ☼ ☼ ☼ ☼

LOOT ☼ ☼ ☼ ☼ ☼

DANGER ☼ ☼ ☼ ☼ ☼

A seemingly ordinary squirrel with night-black fur. A fleeting glance at this animal skittering among the trees wouldn't reveal anything unusual. Watch, however, and you'll see that the black squirrel is a bit larger than its brethren and its fur so dark that it looks like a living shadow. Ironically, while the animal is nocturnal, it craves light—whether the dim glow of a firefly or the blaze of a bonfire, the black squirrel scampers forth to eat it. Though they cannot fly, some claim to have seen black squirrels climb into the sky to nibble on the moon and stars. During the day, they can be found in their dens, greedily staring at the sun. Like common squirrels, they store their food for times of scarcity, burying little nuggets of light in the earth.

Adventurer's Tip: This squirrel is completely harmless. A cache of buried light is a great source of ingredients for alchemists.

The Choctaw people of North America have a legend that solar eclipses are caused by black squirrels trying to eat the sun. Yelling and shooting at the sky would scare away the animals, allowing the sun to regain its full brightness. Completely black animals, especially those of species which are normally otherwise colored, always inspire interest. Black squirrels exist, but they aren't their own species; rather, they are a melanistic variant of ordinary gray or red squirrels with a mutation that causes excess pigment in their skin and fur, turning them black.

Bomb Plant

a.k.a. Exploding Fruit

COMBAT	☼ ☼ ☼ ○ ○	
MAGIC	○ ○ ○ ○ ○	
SMARTS	○ ○ ○ ○ ○	
LOOT	☼ ☼ ○ ○ ○	
DANGER	☼ ☼ ☼ ○ ○	

A cactuslike plant that bears large, round fruit adorned with nasty-looking spikes. Upon ripening, the swollen fruit becomes sensitive to vibrations and, if disturbed, bursts and showers anything nearby with seeds, thorns, and burning pulp, with any victims becoming fertilizer for the next crop. The larger and more brightly colored the fruit, the more sensitive it is, so that even speaking near one can cause it to explode. Due to the short range of the burst, new plants grow around old ones, forming expansive, dangerous patches. While a single fruit may only wound, a chain reaction through a patch can shed enough pulp to burn through steel armor.

Adventurer's Tip: If you must go through an area dense with these plants, throw stones ahead of you to trigger explosions from a safe distance.

> *Plants seeds are usually spread by the wind, clinging to the bodies of animals, or being egested after the fruit is eaten. Some plants spread their seeds though explosive dehiscence—exploding seed pods. Usually the seed pods become very dry and burst from internal strain, propelling the seeds away. In the case of the squirting cucumber, however, the seed pod actually swells with liquid until the pressure causes both liquid and seeds to be ejected.*

Cave Spirit

a.k.a. Karzelek,
Tommyknocker

COMBAT ☼ ☼ ☼ ☼ ☼

MAGIC ☼ ☼ ☼ ☼ ☼

SMARTS ☼ ☼ ☼ ☼ ☼

LOOT ☼ ☼ ☼ ☼ ☼

DANGER ☼ ☼ ☼ ☼ ☼

A strange fairy that lives in caverns and mines, rarely seen but often heard. Since cave spirits never leave their subterranean homes, the only mortals they regularly interact with are miners. Even animals stay near the cavern entrances, refusing to venture into the deeper passages where these creatures live. Like all fairies, the cave spirits' attitude towards mortals is colored by how they are treated. If respected, these beings lead miners to veins rich in metals and gemstones and warn their visitors of imminent danger by knocking on the cave walls. If disrespected (or simply if they're bored), the spirits replace valuable minerals with junk metal, lead miners astray, steal tools, and cause cave-ins. Helpful cave spirits expect to be rewarded for their efforts.

Adventurer's Tip: To ensure safe passage though a cavern, leave a little food for the cave spirits. Even a morsel as small as a crust of bread is appreciated.

Though currently useful for alloys and other chemical processes, cobalt used to be regarded as a useless metal. The metal was named after the kobold, a Germanic cave goblin that was said to replace silver in mines with this mineral. The British Isles have a number of cave spirits, including bluecaps (appearing as blue flames) and knockers (which appear as little miners). Many cultures have caves as entrances to supernatural worlds, where mortals enter never to return.

Centaur

a.k.a. Apotharni

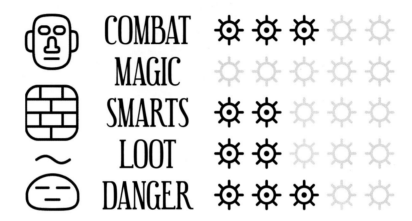

COMBAT ✸✸✸✧✧
MAGIC ✧✧✧✧✧
SMARTS ✸✸✧✧✧
LOOT ✸✸✧✧✧
DANGER ✸✸✸✧✧

A creature with the body of a horse, but where the horse's neck should be, a human torso emerges. How a centaur's internal organs are arranged is a mystery. These hybrid folk are expert skirmishers and archers, skills that they use both when hunting and on the battlefield. They enjoy both the strength and mobility of horses without having to contend with any of the animals' notorious predisposition to panic. A long history of confrontation with humans has made them an insular people that, coupled with their nomadic lifestyle, means they are rarely seen. Even if a centaur develops a friendly relationship with a human, it'll still be loath to allow the person to ride on its back, as centaurs consider this demeaning.

Adventurer's Tip: A centaur's shortbow is comparable in size and range to a human's longbow. One shudders to think the deadly distances a centaur's longbow could reach.

A Greek mythological creature, the children of the god Centaurus and wild mares, they are typically depicted as male, drunken, and rapacious. Female centaurs (centaurides) are mentioned, but rare. Chiron, wiser and more sober than his fellows, was a teacher to many Greek heroes and was transformed in the constellation Centaurus (or Sagittarius) when he died. Similar looking creatures include the Nuckelavee (an evil sea spirit, a horse with a human torso growing out of its back, both flayed) and the Besta Fera (a Brazilian version of the Devil).

Changeling

a.k.a. Fairy Child,
Wechselbalg

COMBAT ☀ ☆ ☆ ☆ ☆
MAGIC ☀ ☀ ☆ ☆ ☆
SMARTS ☀ ☀ ☀ ☆ ☆
LOOT ☀ ☀ ☆ ☆ ☆
DANGER ☀ ☆ ☆ ☆ ☆

A small creature left in cradles by fairies to replace babies they spirit away. Sometimes the changeling is the fairy's true child, other times their elderly and infirm relative. Regardless, the changeling's true family doesn't want to put up with the burden of caring for it and would rather have a precious human newborn. The impostor doesn't seem to mind its abandonment, and relishes the attention it receives from the unsuspecting adoptive parents. The changeling appears to be in a perpetually starving, sickly state, no matter how much it's fed, and rarely stops crying. The mortal family may end up collapsing due to the emotional and financial strain heaped upon them by their false child.

Adventurer's Tip: A changeling can be driven away by forcing it to reveal its true nature. If found out, the changeling will agree to leave and return the true child.

The changeling tale is common in Europe and, like demonic possession and bewitchments, acted as a possible explanation for the existence of children with neurological disorders, physical impediments, or other deviations from standard appearance and behavior. Unfortunately, most methods to rid oneself of the changeling involved horribly abusing the child in the hope that either the changeling would leave or its fairy parents would come to the rescue. Needless to say, no such rescue ever occurred.

Chimera

a.k.a. Hybrid Beast

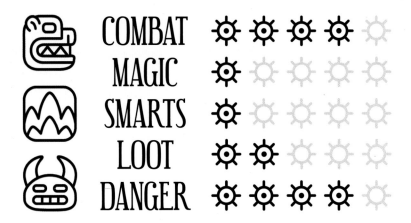

COMBAT ☼ ☼ ☼ ☼ ☼

MAGIC ☼ ☼ ☼ ☼ ☼

SMARTS ☼ ☼ ☼ ☼ ☼

LOOT ☼ ☼ ☼ ☼ ☼

DANGER ☼ ☼ ☼ ☼ ☼

A gruesome hodgepodge of animal parts combined into a single ferocious beast. There are many origins for chimeras, be it breeding between creatures, magical mutation, or accidental creation by the gods from leftover parts. The resultant beast is more ill-tempered and fierce than any of its constituent animals. Their hides are so tough and resistant to magical attacks that they make their dens in places deadly to common creatures, such as volcanoes and acid lakes. Many have developed the ability to breathe fire or poison, which, coupled with their teeth and claws, makes them formidable enemies at both close and long range. Whilst impressive in appearance, the chimera is little more than a dumb animal, though it still seems to show a penchant for cruelty.

Adventurer's Tip: Try to trick each of the chimera's heads into eating metal. The beast's high internal temperature will melt it, blocking off its throats and making it suffocate.

> *The original Chimera was a Greek monster, the daughter of the primordial beings Typhon and Echidna. It's believed that Mount Chimaera, an area of Turkey with vents that expel flammable gas, inspired the creature. In biology, the term is used to describe organisms containing different genotypes. For example, a chimeric organism may have multiple different types of blood cells; patchy pigmentation in their hair, skin, or eyes; or show both male and female physical characteristics.*

Cockatrice

a.k.a. Calcatrix,
Gye-Liong

COMBAT	☀	☀	☼	☼	☼
MAGIC	☀	☀	☀	☼	☼
SMARTS	☀	☼	☼	☼	☼
LOOT	☀	☀	☼	☼	☼
DANGER	☀	☀	☀	☼	☼

A creature hatched from an egg laid by an elderly rooster, incubated under a snake or toad. Though ridiculous in appearance and size (it's little bigger than a chicken), the cockatrice is deadly; its breath and claws are poisonous and its gaze causes paralysis. The animal's short, membranous wings are too weak to allow for prolonged flight, so the cockatrice doesn't stray far from its hatching ground, often a farmhouse. From its burrow, it creeps out at night to feed on the farm's livestock, growing strong and fat while the farmers search for the culprit, until at last the cockatrice grows bold enough to make the farmers its first human victims. As a relative of the basilisk, its greatest foes are weasels, mongooses, and other mustelids.

Adventurer's Tip: The cockatrice has a birdlike fascination with mirrors. Distract it with its own reflection to sneak up on it.

A creature of European folklore, often interchangeable with the basilisk, the main difference being the cockatrice's wings and chicken head. "Cock's eggs," also called "wind eggs," are malformed, yolkless eggs laid by immature hens, but their abnormal appearance led to fears of monstrous spawn. Superstitious farmers will destroy both the egg and the chicken (or suspected cock) that laid it to prevent calamity. Other monstrous chickens are the basan (a Japanese fire-breather), and the aitvaras (a Lithuanian house spirit appearing as a chicken-dragon hybrid).

Colossus

a.k.a. Giant Sentinel,
Mecha

COMBAT ☼ ☼ ☼ ☼ ☼

MAGIC ☼ ☼ ☼ ☼ ☼

SMARTS ☼ ☼ ☼ ☼ ☼

LOOT ☼ ☼ ☼ ☼ ☼

DANGER ☼ ☼ ☼ ☼ ☼

A massive statue that can be animated to fight in battles. A marvel of alchemical engineering, it's so prohibitively expensive that only the richest, most technologically advanced civilizations can afford to build them. The most likely place to find them is near rich temples, massive population centers, and the tombs of god-kings. Colossi can be controlled externally or made to function off a set of predetermined commands, but the inside can be designed to carry at least one pilot. The ruins of some ancient cities are sometimes littered with the remains of these mechanical giants, having been used in some mysterious cataclysmic war. These abandoned colossi may be dangerous, as one that reactivates may still be in combat mode.

Adventurer's Tip: Colossi are capable of causing massive collateral damage. Only use them as a weapon of last resort.

The Colossus of Rhodes was one of the Seven Wonders of the Ancient World, a seventy-cubit-tall (thirty-three meters) statue of the god Helios that stood guard at the city's port. The trope of the giant human-shaped construct is more common in science fiction than fantasy, most notably as the mechas in anime and sentai shows. Notable mechas include the Zords from Power Rangers, *the EVA units from* Neon Genesis Evangelion, *and the Gundams from the various* Gundam *series.*

Crabfolk

a.k.a. Cancerian

COMBAT	☼ ☼ ☼ ○ ○
MAGIC	○ ○ ○ ○ ○
SMARTS	☼ ☼ ○ ○ ○
LOOT	☼ ☼ ○ ○ ○
DANGER	☼ ☼ ○ ○ ○

A race of large sentient crabs, capable of living both on the coast and in the deeper oceans. The crabfolk's heavy claws and shells make them clumsy and ponderously slow, though some have a second set of small claws to allow for more delicate handling. Despite this, crabfolk generally lack the dexterity for any sort of fine crafting and so prize small filigree figures of stone and metal. They acquire these coveted treasures by salvaging from sunken vessels or trading with surface dwellers. Their thick shells means they can withstand the pressure of the ocean's abyss, and they have been known to bring up whalebone and rare minerals from the mysterious depths. Crabfolk, like other sea races, may be in the thrall of forgotten gods that sleep beneath the waves.

Adventurer's Tip: As they grow, crabfolk shed their shells, leaving them soft and vulnerable while the new carapace hardens. The abandoned shells make good base material for armor or shields.

> *Stories of crab monsters are rarer than other sea creatures, but there are certain species that can grow to truly monstrous sizes. The waters around Japan are home to several interesting crabs. Among them is the Japanese spider crab, the world's largest living arthropod, whose outstretched limbs can reach a span of eighteen feet. There is also the heikegani crab (a.k.a. the samurai crab), which has a carapace resembling a scowling human face and is believed to be the reincarnated spirits of defeated Heike warriors.*

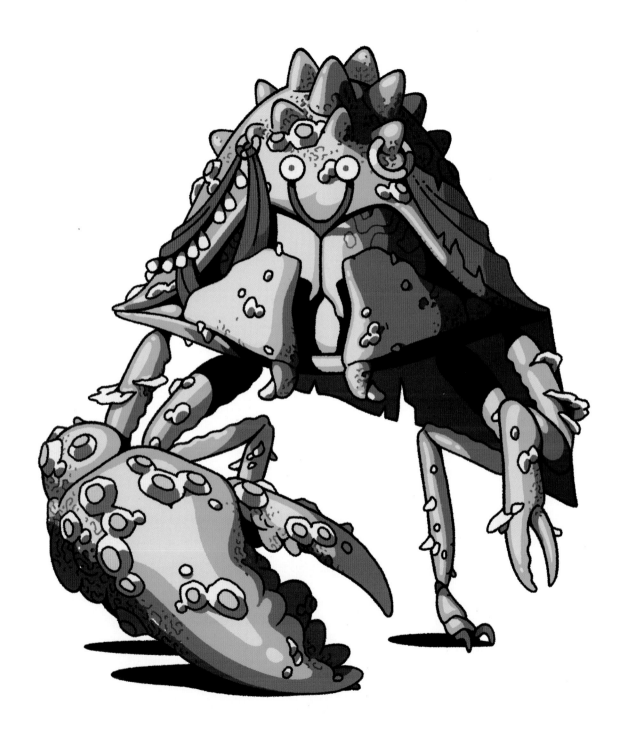

Deerfolk

a.k.a. Cervitaur

COMBAT ✹✹✷✷✷

MAGIC ✹✷✷✷✷

SMARTS ✹✹✹✷✷

LOOT ✹✷✷✷✷

DANGER ✹✹✷✷✷

A relative of the centaur, comparatively small and weak, but much more swift. Both male and female deerfolk have horns—though the males' are more impressive—and their dappled coats blend against the shrubbery and trees of their forest homes. Unlike the warlike centaurs, deerfolk are extremely meek, with any perceived threat making them turn tail and run for cover. Deerfolk are naturally suspicious of anybody who would wander into their territory, and scouts will quietly follow any intruders to determine how dangerous they are. If the trespassers are deemed a hazard, the deerfolk will subtly use calls and tactical rustling to encourage the enemy to walk in a certain direction, leading them into natural hazards like cliffs or the den of an angry bear.

Adventurer's Tip: Their druidic tendencies make deerfolk eager allies to forest spirits, and happily serve them as spies.

> *One of a number of centaurids in modern fantasy culture, which include lions, cows, scorpions, et cetera. While there are some deer- or antelope-human hybrids in mythology and folklore, they tend to either be animalheaded or be bipedal on deer legs. Cernunnos and other Horned God-type nature gods are usually depicted as antlered men. Native North Americans have numerous Deer Woman legends, with her ratio of human-to-deer body parts, true nature, and general attitude towards humanity varying with each story.*

Demon, Disease

a.k.a. Aerico,
Likhoradka

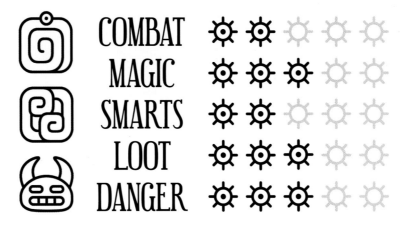

COMBAT	☼	☼	☼	☼	☼
MAGIC	☼	☼	☼	☼	☼
SMARTS	☼	☼	☼	☼	☼
LOOT	☼	☼	☼	☼	☼
DANGER	☼	☼	☼	☼	☼

A demon that specializes in the spread of disease, madness, putrescence, and rot. Minor disease demons only blight individual animals, people, or plants, while the greater of their kind bring nations to their knees by blighting crops and killing in the thousands, leaving cursed and empty cities behind. Disease demons are generally invisible to the naked eye, though their presence can be detected by alternating heat and chills along with a foul smell. When visible, their twisted bodies are dripping with filth and covered in weeping sores. Certain demons specialize in specific diseases, like leprosy, scarlet fever, and the bubonic plague. They can cure as well as sicken, so skilled warlocks and priests can bind these demons and force them to reveal the secrets of medicine.

Adventurer's Tip: Most demons can be driven away by burning rotting offal, but this is useless against these particular spirits. It's better to keep one's environment clean and sweet-smelling.

Before the advent of germ theory, it was believed that sickness was caused by evil spirits or angry gods. Some gods were even in charge of disease and were prayed to for mercy or a cure. In Christianity, the four horsemen of the Apocalypse are said to be War, Famine, Death, and Pestilence. Some scholars list this last rider as Conquest, but since this is seen by many as synonymous with War, Pestilence has become the more popular modern interpretation.

Demon, Imp

a.k.a. Demonic Familiar

COMBAT ✷✷✩✩✩

MAGIC ✷✷✩✩✩

SMARTS ✷✷✷✩✩

LOOT ✷✷✩✩✩

DANGER ✷✷✩✩✩

A type of lesser demon, small in both size and strength. Because of this weakness, imps have to be especially quick and wily to survive the harsh environment that is Hell. These small demons protect themselves by forming pacts with wizards and witches, offering their services as familiars, advisors, and spies. In exchange, their master pledges their soul to the evil powers and sometimes feed the demon on their own blood. The imp's true form is ugly, toothy, and often covered in spikes, scales, and slime, and they disguise themselves as animals such as cats, lizards, and rabbits while in the mortal world. Though not magically potent themselves, they can guide their masters in their pursuits of the dark arts and encourage them down the path of damnation.

Adventurer's Tip: An imp forced to be a familiar is more dangerous than one that offers its services, since they'll gladly turn on their master if given the opportunity.

The term "imp" is given to a wide variety of small supernatural creatures which range from mischievous to malevolent. Their more evil associations may have come from demonizing pagan spirits and folkloric beings. In witch trials, familiars were often used as proof of the accused's evil doings, though the demon in question was usually just a pet or even an empty container which accusers said contained an invisible imp. When the witch was executed, the familiar was often "killed" with them.

Demon, Lesser

a.k.a. Fallen Soul,
Devil, Legion

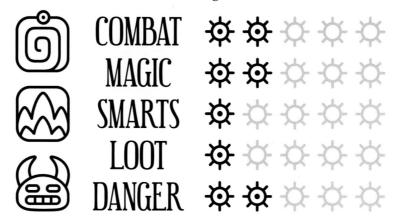

COMBAT	✸ ✸ ✧ ✧ ✧
MAGIC	✸ ✸ ✧ ✧ ✧
SMARTS	✸ ✧ ✧ ✧ ✧
LOOT	✸ ✧ ✧ ✧ ✧
DANGER	✸ ✸ ✧ ✧ ✧

Lesser demons are by far the most common of the infernal hordes, a true case of quantity over quality. They litter the lower circles of Hell, performing grunt work for archdevils, serving as fodder in evil armies, or just trying to avoid getting eaten. It's possible for them to rise through the ranks, but most are held back by an inherent lack of strength, intelligence, or charisma. Like all demons, they enjoy tormenting humans, with lesser demons especially enjoying the chance to be the abuser rather than the victim. On the mortal plane, they'll often claim a higher rank than they have a right to, since only expert priests and warlocks would be able to see through their lies. Unfortunately for the demon, they're easy to trick, and many have found themselves bested by a wily peasant.

Adventurer's Tip: Lesser demons can be driven away by burning incense or rotting offal. A demon that is possessing someone can be driven into a nearby animal, which can then be slaughtered.

> *Outside of a few famous demonic figures (such as Lucifer, Beelzebub, or Mephistopheles), it is assumed that the Underworld is densely populated with hosts of lesser demons. The paintings of Heironymus Bosch often depict fantastic vistas filled with crowds of misshapen demonic figures, and the mystical* Lesser Key of Solomon *catalogues a list of seventy-two archdevils, each served by thousands of underlings. Demon lords in other religions and mythologies are similarly served by lesser demons.*

Demon, Smoke

a.k.a. Enenra

COMBAT ✸ ✸ ☼ ☼ ☼

MAGIC ✸ ✸ ☼ ☼ ☼

SMARTS ✸ ✸ ✸ ☼ ☼

LOOT ✸ ✸ ☼ ☼ ☼

DANGER ✸ ✸ ✸ ☼ ☼

An evil creature made of shifting smoke and noxious vapors. Their bodies are mostly insubstantial, making them difficult to harm with conventional weapons, but they have a small solid core that can be struck to kill them. However, these demons can spread their smoke widely, making it difficult to pinpoint the location of this weak spot. Their favorite method of attack is to swirl around their victims, blinding them and causing coughing fits. When they're inhaled, the demons gleefully shred the victim's throat and lungs with their claws and cause suffocation. Against those who would protect themselves with masks, they can condense their bodies into especially dense, viscous clouds, which can physically entangle and immobilize the target.

Adventurer's Tip: The smoke demon's body is light and airy, even when it condenses itself. A strong wind or heat can cause them to disperse.

> *Demonic creatures were often associated with smoke, fire, mist, and noxious gases, all of which are either dangerous or can leave a person in an isolated, blinded state. While people can burn to death in fires, they more often succumb to smoke inhalation first, since the smoke and hot air cause carbon monoxide poisoning and burn the respiratory passages. Surviving severe smoke inhalation may leave the person with breathing problems for life.*

Doppelganger

a.k.a. Fetch, Twin Stranger,
Vardyvle

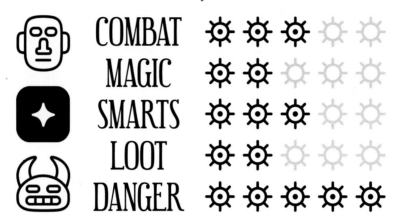

COMBAT ☼ ☼ ☼ ☼ ☼

MAGIC ☼ ☼ ☼ ☼ ☼

SMARTS ☼ ☼ ☼ ☼ ☼

LOOT ☼ ☼ ☼ ☼ ☼

DANGER ☼ ☼ ☼ ☼ ☼

A strange creature able to transform to usurp someone else's life. Dopplegangers are generally born out of a person's shadow or their lack of confidence and fears of mortality. At first amorphous and faded in color, without even a face or sense of self, they steal these things from the first human they see. The doppleganger attaches itself to a particular person, following them, copying them, stealing their memories, and eventually taking over their lives, causing the original person to simply fade away. Some of these creatures steal multiple identities and can take on any of the forms they steal. Spells revealing such a doppleganger's true shape will show it as a roiling mass of faces, weeping and crying to be set free.

Adventurer's Tip: Don't speak to it. Don't look at it. Don't emote near it. Put your affairs in order.

The word doppleganger *("double-walker") first appears in the eighteenth century German novel* Siebenkas, *but the concept of the spirit double is much more ancient. More often than not, it appears as an ill omen, a premonition of someone's death. In real life, a look-alike with no blood relation is possible, but unlikely and eerie. Celebrity lookalikes can find careers as impersonators, and there are websites that allow you to search for your own double. There are as of yet no reports of one usurping the other one's life.*

Dragon, Evil

a.k.a. Wyrm,
Zmey

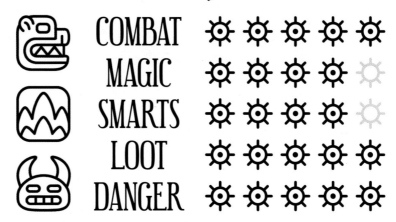

COMBAT	☼ ☼ ☼ ☼ ☼	
MAGIC	☼ ☼ ☼ ☼ ☼	
SMARTS	☼ ☼ ☼ ☼ ☼	
LOOT	☼ ☼ ☼ ☼ ☼	
DANGER	☼ ☼ ☼ ☼ ☼	

A very evil-tempered, intelligent, and dangerous flying beast. The scales of an evil dragon are often red, black, or green, and especially vain dragons decorate themselves with gold and jewels. All dragons are inherently greedy and have a magpie-like fascination for shiny objects, but evil dragons amass especially huge hoards of gold through wanton theft and destruction. Their preferred method is to assault villages with their fiery or acidic breath, extorting riches and food out of the terrified residents. As the dragons get older, they also grow more lazy, spending most of their time sleeping and counting their treasure. They are extremely paranoid and attentive, and a single absent coin from the hoard can send them into a terrible rage.

Adventurer's Tip: The carbuncle, a magical ruby-like gemstone, is found at the center of a dragon's brain. The older the dragon, the bigger and more magical the stone—but, of course, you have to kill the dragon to get it.

In the old folklore and myths of the West, a dragon could be any vaguely reptilian monster. They were generally evil beings and Christians associated them with Satan. The contemporary fantasy dragon is based on Smaug, from J.R.R. Tolkien's The Hobbit. *Smaug himself may have been based on Fafnir, a dwarf of the Icelandic* Volsunga Saga, *who stole his father's treasure and then transformed himself into a dragon to guard it.*

61

Dragon, Good

a.k.a. Celestial Dragon,
Golden Dragon

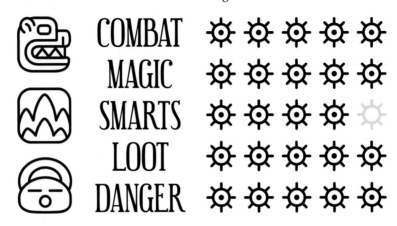

COMBAT	☼ ☼ ☼ ☼ ☼
MAGIC	☼ ☼ ☼ ☼ ☼
SMARTS	☼ ☼ ☼ ☼ ☼
LOOT	☼ ☼ ☼ ☼ ☼
DANGER	☼ ☼ ☼ ☼ ☼

A benevolent beast, having a serpentine body covered in gleaming scales, often gold or some other resplendent color. Their horns are long and graceful and they sport wise whiskers. Like all dragons, their potential for destruction is massive, their greed is boundless, and their pride is unshakable, although good dragons temper these faculties with intelligence and mercy. Highly magical, they occasionally take on human form and walk among men, spreading wisdom and order. When not abroad, they stay in their secluded lairs in mountains, under lakes, or among the clouds, contemplating the mysteries of the universe. In constrast to their evil counterparts, a good dragon's hoard is as likely to be filled with precious art and manuscripts as it is gold and gemstones.

Adventurer's Tip: To get in this dragon's good graces, tell them a new story, present them with a gift, or make flattering comments about their appearance.

While the dragons in Western folklore are generally evil, the dragons in Eastern stories could be evil, neutral, or good, sometimes crossing into divinity. In China, golden or yellow dragons are symbols of good luck and the Imperial dynasty, and the dragon Huang Long brought writing to the mythological Chinese emperor Fu Xi. The dragon remains a popular creature in contemporary fantasy, running the full gamut of intelligence and morality.

Dragon, Hybrid

a.k.a. Dragonborn,
Dragonmen

COMBAT	☼ ☼ ☼ ☼ ☼	
MAGIC	☼ ☼ ☼ ☼ ☼	
SMARTS	☼ ☼ ☼ ☼ ☼	
LOOT	☼ ☼ ☼ ☼ ☼	
DANGER	☼ ☼ ☼ ☼ ☼	

Part dragon, part human, this being is the result of twisted magic or some unnatual union; as such, dragon hybrids can vary accordingly, both mentally and physically. At best, this can result in a bloodline of powerful sorcerers and heroes, destined for leadership and glory, with any overtly draconic features graceful and well-fitting. At worst, they are brutish half-beasts, deformed and dim-witted, seething with volatile rage. Evil dragons, wizards, and demons have been known to create the latter through nefarious magical experiments and use them as heavy infantry in their wicked armies. Dragon hybrids boast both superhuman strength and powerful supernatural abilities, including the ability to breathe fire.

Adventurer's Tip: Each dragon hybrid is a unique foe, but due to their warped physical form many possess at least one weak spot where their hide is thin and easy to pierce—make sure to find it.

Though appearing often in modern fantasy media, this same trope can be found in ancient legends. In Japan, the legendary Emperor Jimmu was said to be descended from the dragon god Ryujin. In Greek mythology, the Ophiogenes were a race of magical healers descended from the human Halia and the dragon Ophiogeneikos. The dragon hybrid in modern fantasy offers characters a measure of monstrous appeal while remaining somewhat humanoid and relatable.

Dragon, Lóng

a.k.a. River Dragon,
Ryu

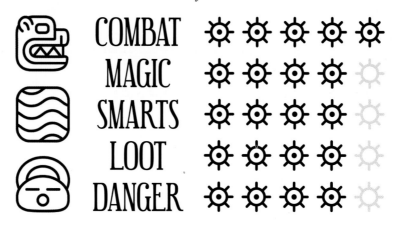

COMBAT	☼ ☼ ☼ ☼ ☼
MAGIC	☼ ☼ ☼ ☼ ○
SMARTS	☼ ☼ ☼ ☼ ○
LOOT	☼ ☼ ☼ ☼ ○
DANGER	☼ ☼ ☼ ☼ ○

A dragon with a sinuous body and mane, of such magical prowess that it crosses over into divinity. The greater lóngs are servants to the gods, and some are even minor deities themselves, ruling over bodies of water and storms. Lóngs may not have always been dragons; some begin life as snakes, fish, or lizards who go on to attain a level of enlightenment that causes them to ascend to dragonhood. Despite not having wings, lóngs are capable of flight, coiling their snakelike bodies as if they were swimming through the air. Lóngs can concentrate their magical powers into pearls, which they carry with them. If a lóng's pearl is stolen, it will lose a portion of its power to the thief who possesses it.

Adventurer's Tip: A dragon pearl grants miraculous powers to mortals who find it, and may even transform them into a dragon themselves.

> *In Eastern culture, dragons (*lóng *in China,* yong *in Korea,* rong *in Vietnam, and* ryu *in Japan) are nature spirits representing fertility and prosperity. Reflecting nature, the dragon could be anything from a destructive force to a magnificent blessing. Dragon kings were generally depicted as living in palaces underwater, though it's often noted that there's breathable air in this realm. Similar domains are common in European fairy folklore.*

Eldritch Horror

a.k.a. Great Old One,
It That Sleeps Beyond The Stars

COMBAT

MAGIC

SMARTS

LOOT

DANGER

An ancient and enigmatic godlike being of which barely anything is known, save perhaps that it is mercifully distant from the realms of man. The eldritch horror is mad and maddening; it appears to those granted visions of it as a vast, bubbling, gibbering mass of hands, eyes, and mouths, as well as other strange organs that defy description. Although likely ignorant or uncaring of humanity, it nevertheless attracts human followers, cultists who seek to hasten its coming with dark rituals and blasphemous acts. Many suspect that it has existed long before our own universe came into being, perhaps as a remnant of some earlier, stranger creation. Its most ardent followers believe its coming will herald the end of worlds.

Adventurer's Tip: Ei-ya! Ei-ya! The old one comes! Rejoice, for the time of reckoning is at hand!

While the twisted cosmology of H.P. Lovecraft was hugely influential in popularizing the idea of ancient alien evils in twentieth century storytelling, the act of caricaturing foreign religions as insidious and secretive cults in the thrall of dark gods is universal and longstanding (particularly when accompanied by racist rhetoric). The use of slimy, amorphous, or tentacular imagery in the descriptions of Lovecraft's creations calls to mind the bodies of deep-sea cephalopods like the giant squid, creatures which seem thoroughly alien to our mammalian sensibilities.

Elemental, Air

a.k.a. Air Spirit,
Sylph

COMBAT	☀	☼	☼	☼	☼
MAGIC	☀	☼	☼	☼	☼
SMARTS	☀	☀	☼	☼	☼
LOOT	☀	☀	☼	☼	☼
DANGER	☀	☀	☼	☼	☼

A living manifestation of air, the fastest of the four elements. Despite the air elemental's speed, its light body has very little in the way of physical strength. Because of this, most of them are no more inconvenient than a mild breeze, only capable of blowing up dust or scattering paper. However, a large air elemental is as powerful as a hurricane and accompanied by thunderous wailing. They are often invisible but can take on a visible shape, generally appearing cloudy and pale but with great malleability, able to inflate themselves as they prepare an especially strong puff of wind. Air elementals can work together with fire and water elementals to form storms, but have little to no influence on earth elementals.

Adventurer's Tip: A persistent wind that keeps blowing away important items or raising dust may be an air elemental having fun at your expense.

Before modern chemistry, many cultures broke down the makeup of the universe into the basic elements of Air, Earth, Fire, and Water, sometimes including a mysterious fifth element. Everything was comprised of a mixture of all four elements, and imbalances were thought to cause disaster or disease. Air is absent from the Chinese element system, replaced by Wood and Metal. In this system, its closest equivalent is Qi (life energy) or Void (the perfect, immutable aspects of the universe).

Elemental, Earth

a.k.a. Earth Spirit,
Terran

COMBAT ☼ ☼ ☼ ☼ ☼

MAGIC ☼ ☼ ☼ ☼ ☼

SMARTS ☼ ☼ ☼ ☼ ☼

LOOT ☼ ☼ ☼ ☼ ☼

DANGER ☼ ☼ ☼ ☼ ☼

A living manifestation of earth, the most stable of the four elements. Though slow and lumbering when overground, it can swim though packed earth like a fish through water. Small earth elementals are as small as pebbles but can grow to the size of mountains. Loath to move and in a near-constant dormant state, vegetation easily grows on them, fusing them into the landscape. Because of this excellent camouflage, it is easy to enrage an earth elemental by mining into what you honestly assumed was a mountain. The upset elemental may set off a chain of earthquakes, cave-ins, and landslides which will uproot and bury any nearby settlements. Though they can blend with water and fire elementals to create mud and lava, the results are still slow-moving.

Adventurer's Tip: Earth elementals make for good guardians, being strong, patient, tough, and not given to wanderlust like other elementals.

> *The four living physical representations of the Classical elements were put forth by Paracelsus, a sixteenth century alchemist: airy sylphs, earthy gnomes, fiery salamanders, and watery undines. The idea isn't unique to him, since animistic mythologies had already assigned physical bodies to natural spirits. The elemental creature continues today as a common trope in fantasy media. However, we now know that there aren't four elements but over a hundred, each defined by its atomic weight.*

Elemental, Fire

a.k.a. Fire Spirit

COMBAT ☼ ☼ ☼ ☼ ☼

MAGIC ☼ ☼ ☼ ☼ ☼

SMARTS ☼ ☼ ☼ ☼ ☼

LOOT ☼ ☼ ☼ ☼ ☼

DANGER ☼ ☼ ☼ ☼ ☼

A living manifestation of fire, the most destructive of the four elements. They are the second fastest next to air elementals, but a good deal more ill-tempered. Even the smallest of their kind, little bigger than a spark, can set off conflagrations, killing and/or displacing hundreds if not thousands of creatures. Large fire elementals appear as horrifying masses of flames, rolling across the landscape, leaving a charred wasteland in their wake. Like all elementals, they aren't evil, but their difficulty controlling their heat means that even benign individuals can cause damage without meaning to. Fire elementals may blend with air and earth elementals to create storms and volcanoes; in contact with water elementals, they neutralize each other.

Adventurer's Tip: It's inadvisable to work with fire elementals above a certain size. Small elementals can be bound to a blacksmith's forge and will imbue any armor or weapons worked there with magical powers.

The Classical elements have their chemical parallel in the four fundamental states of matter: air for gaseous, water for liquid, earth for solid, and fire for plasma. Plasma is created when gas is heated, causing its atoms to lose electrons, a process called ionization, giving rise to phenomena such as lightning and stars. Another process associated with the element of fire would be combustion, a chemical reaction where energy is released in the form of light and heat.

Elemental, Water

a.k.a. Water Spirit

COMBAT	☀	☀	☼	☼	☼
MAGIC	☀	☼	☼	☼	☼
SMARTS	☀	☀	☼	☼	☼
LOOT	☀	☀	☼	☼	☼
DANGER	☀	☀	☼	☼	☼

A living manifestation of water, the most flexible of the four elements. As with the air elemental, they are often mischievous and small ones are largely harmless. They are of a fickle nature, so their destructive urges are tempered with kindly ones; a water elemental is as likely to scuttle a ship as it is to carry a drowning person to safety. Sometimes water elementals can be seen with colonies of fish and other aquatic creatures living in their bodies, much how an earth elemental may be overgrown with plant life. They have been known to either serve or be served by water dragons, merfolk, and similar sentient creatures. These elementals are very resilient, being able to exist as ice and vapor.

Adventurer's Tip: Often blending in with surrounding waters, this elemental can be hard to spot. Keep an eye out for currents that seem to run counter to the tides.

> *The state of matter of an element is defined by the mobility of its atomic structure and can be changed by adding or removing energy (i.e. heating or cooling). Solids exist at an element's coolest state, becoming liquid, gas, or plasma as more energy is added. There are other states of matter, but these are either present under very extreme conditions or theoretical. Though living things are treated as solid, they're mostly composed of water. Does this mean humans are water elementals?*

Enlightened One

a.k.a. Bodhisattva,
Hermit

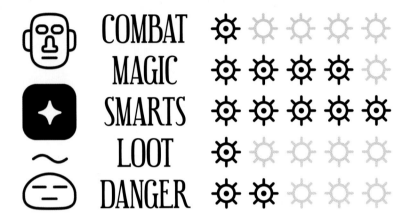

COMBAT	☀	☆	☆	☆	☆
MAGIC	☀	☀	☀	☀	☆
SMARTS	☀	☀	☀	☀	☀
LOOT	☀	☆	☆	☆	☆
DANGER	☀	☀	☆	☆	☆

Once a mere human, this being has transcended after gaining greater insight into the workings of the universe. The enlightened ones have been touched by some divine knowledge, altering them both mentally and physically. Seeing beyond the petty needs of common mortals, these people generally live in isolated places or on the outskirts of society, alone with their contemplations. They can grow very thin, as they abstain from food or drink, sustaining themselves instead off the energy of the universe. Should they deign to speak, the words of an enlightened one can sound nonsensical or contradictory, but they may reveal divine truths. To most people, they are madmen; to their followers, they are the voice of the gods.

Adventurer's Tip: The advice of an enlightened one is seldom understood right away, sometimes only becoming relevant in some dire situation.

> *The concept of a person having spiritual insight which elevates them over common men is present in all religions, both present and past. Though most religious orders live a life separate from the secular, some believers take it to an extreme that completely cuts them off from normal society. In Buddhism and Hinduism, true enlightenment is said to free one from the cycle of reincarnation, the shackles of having to endure the pain and indignities of material life, and allow one to exist in a constant perfect state of nothingness.*

79

Ettin

a.k.a. Polycephalon

COMBAT ☼ ☼ ☼ ☼ ☼

MAGIC ☼ ☼ ☼ ☼ ☼

SMARTS ☼ ☼ ☼ ☼ ☼

LOOT ☼ ☼ ☼ ☼ ☼

DANGER ☼ ☼ ☼ ☼ ☼

Rather than an independent species, ettin is an umbrella term for mutant, multi-headed giants. Generally, each head has its own personality and, as many giants are short-tempered and violent, explosive arguments can erupt between them. Even though they share the same body, these disagreements can quickly become physical, resulting in ettins' notoriously short lifespans. An ettin who can control its destructive impulses, or even have its heads exist harmoniously, can become insightful and clever, engaging in long debates with itself and delighting in tricking travellers with riddles. Even a stupid ettin is a desirable asset for a warlord if it's properly managed; the heads needn't sleep at the same time, making them excellent sentries.

Adventurer's Tip: Confuse and anger an ettin by complementing one of the heads, driving the other ones into fits of jealous rage.

Multi-headed giants, demons, and other creatures are common throughout world folklore and mythology. The word "ettin" may be a corruption of jötunn, *a Scandinavian term for giant. Polycephaly is a real-life medical condition, resulting in two or more heads on one body (each its own person), with possible duplicate organs or body parts. Diprosopus is a similar condition, where multiple faces merge on one head. The lifespan of people with polycephaly or diprosopus may be compromised by the malformation of vital organs.*

Fairy Monarch

a.k.a. Elf King,
Green Man

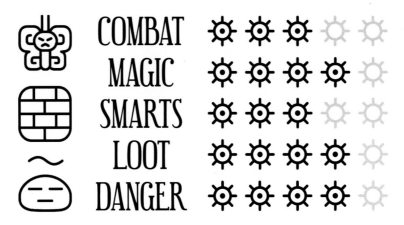

COMBAT	☼	☼	☼	☼	☼
MAGIC	☼	☼	☼	☼	☼
SMARTS	☼	☼	☼	☼	☼
LOOT	☼	☼	☼	☼	☼
DANGER	☼	☼	☼	☼	☼

The kings and queens of fairykind, who rule from palaces built underground, in the midst of ruins, underwater, or in magical groves. The fairy monarch is spiritually tied to its domain, so that the good or evil of the ruling fairy is reflected in the wholesomeness and beauty of its kingdom. Their magic and control over the environment make these royals exist on a level akin to minor deities; they thus have the compounded aloofness of both fairykind and aristocracy, and expect everything to be done their way. They enjoy bringing mortals into their world, whether as lovers or slaves, and cannot understand why anyone would want to leave. Time flows differently in the fairy kingdoms, so that an hour there can last anywhere between seconds and years in the mortal world.

Adventurer's Tip: The magic of most fairies can be neutralized by iron. A knife in a gateway can be used to keep passages between mortal and fairy domains open.

Fairies and fairy lords may be the gods of old polytheistic religions demoted into folktales by the spread of more powerful monotheistic faiths. Greco-Roman, Norse, and Celtic mythologies are rife with stories showing the gods as powerful, proud, and petty, much how fairy monarchs are depicted in early legends. Famous literary depictions include Titania and Oberon (immortalized by Shakespeare's A Midsummer Night's Dream*), Morgan le Fay of Arthurian legend, and the various witches and queens featured in L. Frank Baum's* Land of Oz *series.*

Fairy, Flower

a.k.a Leshy,
Pixie

COMBAT ☼ ☆ ☆ ☆ ☆
MAGIC ☼ ☼ ☆ ☆ ☆
SMARTS ☼ ☼ ☼ ☆ ☆
LOOT ☼ ☆ ☆ ☆ ☆
DANGER ☼ ☆ ☆ ☆ ☆

A very small fairy, having leaf or petallike hair or wings. Like many of the Good People, flower fairies are mischievous, but their tricks are relatively harmless compared to the greater members of their kind. They enjoy turning invisible to bother mortals, stealing small items here and there, or pricking them with needles. A favorite game is to shed fairy dust on travellers, a glittering powder with soporific qualities, and stealing the sleeper's clothes, covering them in garlands, and tangling up their hair with knots. When these small fairies sleep, they turn into flowers, shedding their petal cocoons when they wake up. Their nature means that flower fairies are most active during the spring and disappear during the winter.

Adventurer's Tip: Though they like to steal, fairies have little use for mortal items. Once they get bored of their toys, they hide them somewhere nearby.

Fairies were originally fearsome, eerie creatures, as dangerous as the wild they represented. As nature was tamed, so depictions of fairies became gentle and safe. The modern saccharine butterfly-and-flower form of these creatures is especially notable in the early twentieth century with Cicely Mary Barker's Flower Fairy *book series. Belief in fairies persisted for a long time—in 1917 the Cottingley Fairies hoax, a series of photographs of young girls with "fairies" (actually card cutouts), duped many people, including author and spiritualist Sir Arthur Conan Doyle.*

Fairy, Snow

a.k.a. Marzanna,
Winter Spirit

COMBAT ☼ ☼ ☼ ☼ ☼
MAGIC ☼ ☼ ☼ ☼ ☼
SMARTS ☼ ☼ ☼ ☼ ☼
LOOT ☼ ☼ ☼ ☼ ☼
DANGER ☼ ☼ ☼ ☼ ☼

A fairy native to cold weather, travelling with the winter season or living in lands perpetually buried in snow. Though some bedeck themselves in fur like mortal nobility, snow fairies radiate no warmth. They are most active at night, drawing frost on windows and leaves and freezing water beneath their feet. They are especially blind to the needs of others, finding their icy creations beautiful and not understanding the harm that cold can do to living things. Mortals who take the snow fairies' fancy slowly lose their capacity for empathy as their hearts freeze. The monarchs of the snow fairies build their palaces out of snow and ice, decorating them with the fractal patterns of snowflakes.

Adventurer's Tip: Snow fairies find the light of fire beautiful but are terrified by its heat.

Snow and winter spirits are most common in countries with long or harsh winters. In older times, these spirits were seen as dangerous, since the dark, barren winter months weren't a happy time. As indoor heating, reliable food production, and industrialization became better managed and more commonplace, the image of snow spirits has softened somewhat, allowing them to represent winter fun and the beauty of ice and snow. Hans Christian Andersen's eponymous character in The Snow Queen *is a good example of this creature, being beautiful, curious, and uncaring.*

Feathered Serpent

a.k.a. Couatl,
Feathered Dragon

COMBAT	☼	☼	☼	☼	☀
MAGIC	☼	☼	☼	☼	☀
SMARTS	☼	☼	☼	☼	☀
LOOT	☼	☼	☼	☼	☀
DANGER	☼	☼	☼	☼	☀

A gigantic flying snake covered in colorful plumes, primarily found in tropical climates. The feathered serpent is a relative of dragons; it is most like the Lóng Dragon, both being long-bodied and having divine powers. The plumes of the serpent are most luxurious around the head and become small and scalelike along the body. This serpent has a great depth of knowledge, strong magic, and can influence the weather, powers which it is glad to share with lesser creatures, especially those who would treat it as a god. In exchange for its gifts, the snake receives praise and sacrifices, be they vegetable, animal, or human. When it is their time to die, the feathered serpents fly into the sky and transform into stardust.

Adventurer's Tip: Though they may eat humans, feathered serpents will not accept a virtuous human as a sacrifice, preferring to use its teeth to punish the wicked.

> *Of the many feathered serpent gods in the Americas, Quetzalcoatl of the Aztecs is the best known. He is generally considered one of the less bloodthirsty gods in a religion rife with human sacrifice. Some creation myths have him reviving the people that populate the Fifth Sun (this world) using the bones of the dead from the previous four creations. Dinosaur fossils are thought to have inspired stories of dragons, and since the 1990s it is accepted that some of these ancient animals were feathered.*

Fire Bat

a.k.a. Spark Bat

COMBAT	☼ ☼ ☼ ☼ ☼
MAGIC	☼ ☼ ☼ ☼ ☼
SMARTS	☼ ☼ ☼ ☼ ☼
LOOT	☼ ☼ ☼ ☼ ☼
DANGER	☼ ☼ ☼ ☼ ☼

A bat wreathed in supernatural fire, common in magic caves and volcanic caverns. This creature is one of many animals mutated by the elemental magic of their environment. When roosting, their bodies are dark, blending into their rocky surroundings with only a faint red glow beneath their wings giving them away. When disturbed, the whole colony takes flight, lighting up in a blazing panic. The same magic that influenced the creation of this species also imbued them with an especially vicious territorial streak and an intelligence that allows them to pinpoint flammable materials. An ordinary cave of bats is already a nuisance to adventurers, but one that can immolate one's clothing, baggage, and spellbooks is another thing altogether.

Adventurer's Tip: Fire bats (and all other creatures that are so strongly linked with the element of fire) can be repelled with water or cold magic.

Fire is commonly linked with various monsters, either as a destructive force (dragons, demons, chimerae, etc. . . .) or as a sign of life-giving divinity (angels, ifrits, firebirds . . .). Adding an aspect of fire—or another classical element for that matter—is an easy way to make any mundane creature more fantastical. Fire keese, the fiery version of a batlike enemy in The Legend of Zelda *series, appear as a small enemy in many games. Though they generally die after one hit, it can still mean the end for your wooden shield.*

Ghost

a.k.a. Phantom,
Specter

COMBAT					
MAGIC	✸	✸	✸		
SMARTS	✸	✸			
LOOT	✸	✸			
DANGER	✸	✸	✸		

The bodiless souls of the dead, lingering on the earthly plane. Ghosts are made by the strong emotions a person felt at the moment of their death, normally fear, anger, pain, or longing, making them unable or unwilling to pass on to the next world. Because of their inherent inability to exist harmoniously in the world of the living, they suck the heat out of the air, bring the smell of rotting corpses, cause items to break, and bring nightmares. The sight of a ghost is enough to strike the living with fear-induced paralysis—this is particularly unfortunate if the ghost needs a living person's assistance in order to move on. Animals, children, and the magically gifted, all more in tune with the psychic world, are especially sensitive to the presence of ghosts.

Adventurer's Tip: Ghosts can be repelled with prayer and magic symbols, but in many cases it is more constructive to help the spirit attain peace than try to fight it.

> *All cultures have stories of the dead coming back to haunt the living. In Cornwall, England, there's the famous legend of Jan Tregeagle, a miserable landlord. After he dies, his spirit is raised from the dead to settle a legal dispute with his tenants, and he refuses to go back to Hell when the problem is resolved. He haunts various locales and is so stubborn that neither priests, saints, nor angels could exorcise him. Eventually he is allowed to stay on Earth, but bound to perform impossible tasks until Judgment Day.*

Ghost Wizard

a.k.a. Wizard Ghost

COMBAT
MAGIC
SMARTS
LOOT
DANGER

A wizard, psychic, or other arcane dabbler who has accidentally stumbled into undeath. Those who take up magical vocations run a greater risk of becoming ghosts than the average person, whether by faulty spellcasting, astral projection gone awry, or simply an unhealthy commitment to study. The ghost of a wizard retains much of the power it had in life, but is limited by the fact that it can't leave its place of death and may even be bound to magical items it once used, such as wands and spellbooks. People who come into ownership of these items can find themselves with a powerful magic tutor, though the ghost may attempt to manipulate their student and take possession of their body.

Adventurer's Tip: Do your research before entering the deserted lair of a mysteriously disappeared wizard and don't interact with any ominous tomes or glowing symbols.

> *This is as the normal ghost, but with added magical powers, much how a lich can be interpreted as a zombie wizard. The* Harry Potter *series has several examples of this: Professor Binns as a wizard that forgot to pass on, Voldemort as a displaced soul, and Dumbledore as a spectral advisor. Science fiction stories sometimes feature ghostlike figures as spirit advisors, such as the force ghosts of Obi-Wan Kenobi and Yoda in* Star Wars.

Ghoul

a.k.a. Cursed Cannibal,
Ghûl

COMBAT ⚙ ⚙ ☼ ☼ ☼
MAGIC ⚙ ☼ ☼ ☼ ☼
SMARTS ⚙ ⚙ ☼ ☼ ☼
LOOT ⚙ ⚙ ☼ ☼ ☼
DANGER ⚙ ⚙ ☼ ☼ ☼

A person who practiced cannibalism in life, transformed into a monster after death. Newly formed ghouls appear human, but the longer they persist, the more bestial they become, both in mind and body, losing their living memories and becoming incapable of speech. Packs of these fiends live in sprawling, ill-smelling warrens that connect to graveyards, charnel pits, and battlefields, ensuring a steady supply of rotten corpses. Ghouls generally stay away from the living, preferring to scavenge, but they'll gladly accept the company of any person who shares their culinary tastes. The claws and teeth of these monsters are riddled with disease due to the flecks of decayed flesh thereon, so any wound they give can quickly turn septic.

Adventurer's Tip: If a corpse goes missing but precious jewelery has been left behind, the culprit may be a ghoul rather than a graverobber.

The name is derived from the Arabic word ghala *("to seize"). The original pre-Islamic* ghûl *or* gallu *was a shapeshifting desert jinn, often female, which would lure and kill travellers. Later European translations of Arabic texts changed them to graverobbing undead, the interpretation that remains most popular today. The term "ghoul" is often applied to any undead, especially those who feed on humans, such as vampires and zombies.*

Giant Lizard

a.k.a. Dinosaur,
Pseudodragon

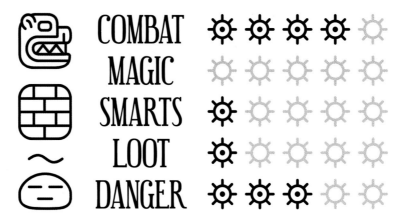

COMBAT ☼ ☼ ☼ ☼ ☼
MAGIC ☼ ☼ ☼ ☼ ☼
SMARTS ☼ ☼ ☼ ☼ ☼
LOOT ☼ ☼ ☼ ☼ ☼
DANGER ☼ ☼ ☼ ☼ ☼

A massive reptile dwelling in deserts, jungles, and the secret lush world underneath the planet's crust. It's said that giant lizards were plentiful in the past, a time when serpentfolk and other reptiles dominated the world. Legends tell of a cataclysmic event that caused their numbers to dwindle, allowing other life-forms to flourish. Giant lizards come in a variety of shapes and sizes, being either as small as dogs or big as houses, bipedal or quadrupedal, having dull-colored hides or ostentatious frills and featherlike scales. Though these beasts can be easily mistaken for dragons, they are mere dumb animals, caring only for eating, sleeping, and finding warm patches of sunshine to bask in.

Adventurer's Tip: A slumbering lizard's scaly hide is easily mistaken for rocky ground beneath the feet, so tread carefully.

> *Giant mythological lizard-monsters and dragons are likely inspired by real animals, both the bones of the extinct and sightings of the current. Komodo dragons and monitor lizards can reach three meters in length, and some crocodiles (if they don't succumb to disease or other predators) continue growing throughout their lives. The largest crocodile measured to date is Lolong, a saltwater crocodile from the Philippines, who measured over six meters and weighed over a ton when he was captured in 2011.*

Giant, Frost

a.k.a. Jötunn,
Rime Giant

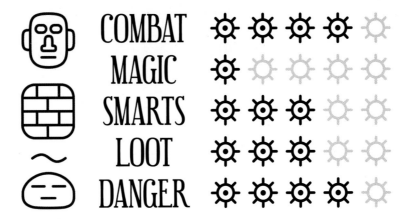

COMBAT	☀	☀	☀	☀	☼
MAGIC	☀	☼	☼	☼	☼
SMARTS	☀	☀	☀	☼	☼
LOOT	☀	☀	☀	☼	☼
DANGER	☀	☀	☀	☀	☼

Once a member of a primordial titan race, pushed to the cold wastelands at the edges of the world by the arrival of newer deities. Though frost giants may wear furs or boast of long, dense beards, they don't feel the cold; these accoutrements are for fashion and status, not practical purposes. These dwellers of the perpetually frozen countries are mighty warriors and hunters, and often keep massive warhounds, wolves, bears, and eagles as companions. Some giants take up a more peaceful life of shepherding, herding great sheep, elk, and musk oxen the way a human farmer might keep chickens. Their leaders boast magical wisdom, granting them the ability to transform into animals or wind, create mist, or raise mountains.

Adventurer's Tip: A giant is still dangerous from a distance, as they can pick up massive boulders and hurl them at human intruders.

> *From Norse mythology, frost giants (jötunn) lived in Jötunheimr, one of the nine worlds of Norse cosmology. Their ancestor, the primeval Ymir, was killed by the Aesir, the Norse gods, and his corpse was used to make the world. The conflict between primordial giants and new gods is reflected in many mythologies (the titans and giants versus the Greek gods, the fomorians versus the Irish gods . . .), often symbolizing taming of nature by civilization or the inevitable destruction of old ways and traditions.*

Giant, Storm

a.k.a. Cloud Giant

COMBAT	☼ ☼ ☼ ☼ ○
MAGIC	☼ ☼ ☼ ○ ○
SMARTS	☼ ☼ ○ ○ ○
LOOT	☼ ☼ ☼ ○ ○
DANGER	☼ ☼ ☼ ☼ ○

Once a member of a primordial titan race, pushed to unreachable mountain peaks and the sky by the arrival of newer deities. Storm giants are not affected by the cold and thin air of their environment and, despite their great size and weight, they're capable of walking on clouds without sinking through them. As their name implies, storm giant magic revolves around weather control, and they are able to stir up tempests, wield lightning, and manipulate the heavenly bodies. They can make clouds and wind solid, using them as building materials for their sky castles. Should avalanches and thunder not deter the enemies entering their realms, the giants may ride down on the backs of giant eagles and war-clouds to smite them.

Adventurer's Tip: If you plan to steal from a storm giant, be sure to well prepare your escape—it's a long way down from up there.

Many nations from around the world have their own versions of the sky-dwelling thunder god. Some are depicted as monstrous and dangerous (like devillike Raijin of Japanese mythology), while other times their powers are symbolic of authority and strength (like Zeus, chief of the Greek gods). These gods may have become the violent giants of modern European folklore, as Christianity dismantled the older polytheistic religions. The giant of the fairy tale Jack and the Beanstalk *lived in a castle in the clouds.*

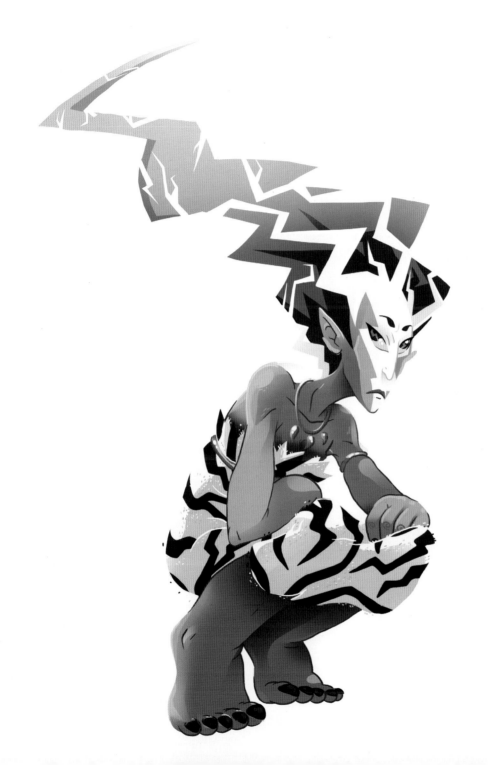

Gnoll

a.k.a. Bultungin,
Kaftar

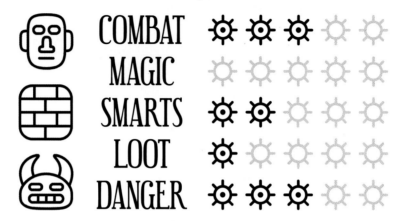

COMBAT ☼ ☼ ☼ ☀ ☀
MAGIC ☀ ☀ ☀ ☀ ☀
SMARTS ☼ ☼ ☀ ☀ ☀
LOOT ☼ ☀ ☀ ☀ ☀
DANGER ☼ ☼ ☼ ☀ ☀

A humanoid with the features of a hyena, its fur matted with blood, evil in appearance, smell, and thought. Gnolls live in chaotic groups led by the fiercest and most cruel among them. The position of leader constantly shifts due to in-fighting, as old leaders are challenged, killed, and eaten by stronger and younger pack members. These customs lead to gnolls having extremely short lifespans, as almost none survive to old age. These beasts are obligate carnivores and care little for the source of their meat. Where weak packs survive by scavenging, strong packs delight in ambushing villages to steal away fresh, screaming meat and slaves. It's uncertain whether gnolls are closer to cursed humans or ascended hyenas.

Adventurer's Tip: A diet often consisting of spoiled flesh has led to gnolls developing strong constitutions, making them immune to most diseases and poisons.

Originally a hybrid between a gnome and troll, created by the Irish writer Lord Dunsany. It was transformed into a hyena-man in the Dungeons & Dragons *game, possibly influenced by African were-hyena myths. The areas of Chad, Somalia, and Ethiopia have stories where witches and blacksmiths would transform themselves into hyenas at night to attack and eat humans. These stories follow a similar pattern to the European werewolf myth.*

Goblin

a.k.a. Hobgoblin

COMBAT ☀ ☼ ☼ ☼ ☼
MAGIC ☼ ☼ ☼ ☼ ☼
SMARTS ☀ ☀ ☼ ☼ ☼
LOOT ☀ ☼ ☼ ☼ ☼
DANGER ☀ ☀ ☼ ☼ ☼

A race of small, grotesque humanoids, goblins are raucous, belligerent, and unpleasant. Ironically, despite being predisposed to chaos, they are gifted in the notoriously tricky fields of alchemy and engineering, which they gear towards their greatest love: destruction. Goblins are especially fond of explosions, the bigger and more fiery the better. Chief engineers will recruit dozens of their fellows in these scientific endeavors, tinkering with acids, metals, steam power, explosives, electricity, and so on. This crazed genius makes goblin technology a slapdash affair at best, as dangerous to its creators as to their enemies. This isn't seen as a flaw by the creatures themselves, since by the end of the day someone has been stabbed, mangled, or blown up.

Adventurer's Tip: Goblin blueprints are seldom worthwhile, as the fact that most can't function without self-destructing is part of the design.

The term "goblins" was originally applied to a number of small fairies or demonic creatures from European folklore. J.R.R. Tolkien's Lord of the Rings *series popularized the interpretation of goblins as a race of barbaric beings. In his stories, they act as an evil counterpart to dwarves, both peoples being small subterranean warriors gifted in crafting. This type of goblin remains a popular enemy in fantasy media, especially as low-level minions in games.*

Golem, Iron

a.k.a. Android,
Robot

COMBAT	☼ ☼ ☼ ☼ ☼
MAGIC	☼ ☼ ☼ ☼ ☼
SMARTS	☼ ☼ ☼ ☼ ☼
LOOT	☼ ☼ ☼ ☼ ☼
DANGER	☼ ☼ ☼ ☼ ☼

A metal statue animated by magic or alchemy. The majority of iron golems are mindless drones, only capable of carrying out a finite number of tasks. However, accomplished wizards will seal a spirit inside the metal husk, imbuing their creation with greater intelligence, but at the risk having the golem acquire self-awareness. The typical iron golem is humanoid, much like a walking suit of armour, but they can be built in any shape. Craftsmen rich in materials, time, and talent may replace their human staff with these creations, having them act as servants, entertainers, and guards. Iron and steel are good base materials, making the golem strong and resilient but slow and clumsy. The iron can be replaced with prettier, softer metals if the golem isn't meant for combat.

Adventurer's Tip: Always build a remote kill-switch into your golem, as malfunctions can be disastrous.

The original golem is a being of Jewish folklore, a giant figure of clay animated by inscribing holy words on or within it. The term has since been adopted into fantasy literature, acting as a catchall term for all sorts of humanoid constructs and robotic servants. Real-life attempts to make automata have a long history, with designs appearing as early as the first century. Non-anthropomorphic robots are common in modern manufacturing industries, but human- and animal-shaped ones have yet to find a role beyond gimmickry.

Golem, Snow

a.k.a. Snowman

COMBAT ✸ ✸ ✦ ✦ ✦
MAGIC ✸ ✸ ✦ ✦ ✦
SMARTS ✦ ✦ ✦ ✦ ✦
LOOT ✸ ✦ ✦ ✦ ✦
DANGER ✸ ✸ ✸ ✦ ✦

A magical being made entirely of snow, brought to life either with intent or by accident. They can be constructed deliberately by spellcasters, following the typical golem model of being big, strong, and mindless. However, they can also be animated spontaneously by the wishes of the innocent; these tend to be small, peaceful, and independent (though naïve). So long as they live in a location with plenty of snow, these golems are effectively immune to damage, as they're able to self-repair by packing new snow onto the damaged area. This magical protection does little to guard them against melting and, though they may be able to smother smaller flames, continuous exposure to heat damages them at too fast a rate to repair.

Adventurer's Tip: Snow fairies are especially fond of creating these golems, using them as servants and guards in their ice palaces.

One of the most recognizable symbols of winter fun, with the earliest supposed image of a snowman appearing in the fourteenth century Book of Hours. *Sentient snowmen appear later, such as in Hans Christian Andersen's 1861 short story* The Snowman. *Arguably the most well-known snowman from the twentieth century is Frosty the Snowman. At first a character in an American song from 1950, he later went on to star in numerous films and TV shows.*

Golem, Skeletal

a.k.a. Bone Golem

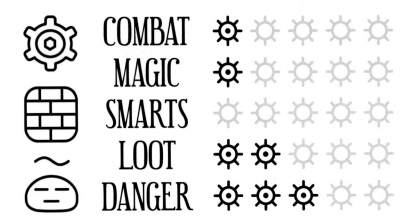

COMBAT	☀	☆	☆	☆	☆
MAGIC	☀	☆	☆	☆	☆
SMARTS	☆	☆	☆	☆	☆
LOOT	☀	☀	☆	☆	☆
DANGER	☀	☀	☀	☆	☆

Though the skeletal golem may appear undead, it is technically a construct—an unthinking automaton built by necromancers. These monstrosities offer an extra element of psychological warfare that other golems do not provide: the horror of a watching a hideous jumble of bones move about. Creative wizards (or simply those running low on whole skeletons) will cobble them together using the bones of many different creatures—with varying results. These creations run the gamut between horrifying and efficient skeletal chimerae to pathetic, misshapen structures barely able to propel themselves. The structural integrity of the bones is weak, even when bolstered with magic, but skeletal golems are easy to reassemble and don't have the carrion smell of zombies.

Adventurer's Tip: Don't make skeleton golems from birds. Their hollow bones are even weaker than ordinary bones, and the extra magic required to make them fly isn't worth the effort.

Grim creations such as this are a popular choice for necromantic villains. The desecration of dead bodies (and their use in dark rituals) is a deeply uncomfortable concept in most societies, and many traditional horror stories center around this taboo. The undead and golems make excellent enemies for game creators who don't want to burden their players with the moral quandary of killing sentient creatures.

Gorgon

a.k.a. Dreadful One,
Medusa

COMBAT	☼ ☼ ☼ ☼ ☼
MAGIC	☼ ☼ ☼ ☼ ☼
SMARTS	☼ ☼ ☼ ☼ ☼
LOOT	☼ ☼ ☼ ☼ ☼
DANGER	☼ ☼ ☼ ☼ ☼

Women cursed into a hideous form by the gods, often punished for some act of sacrilege. The gorgons' bodies are covered in hard scales, their hair is a writhing tangle of venomous snakes, and their faces are too ugly to behold. Their very blood carries the taint of their curse, with the shed drops causing serpents to erupt from the earth. Gorgons lives in ruins and caves, imprisoned there by feelings of loathing, fear, and shame, with only each other for company. The gorgon is so horrifying that the mere sight of it causes any beholder to turn to stone. They cannot control this ability, and gazing upon a dead gorgon yields the same results as a live one. Their isolated lairs are strewn with the stony remains of those foolish or unlucky enough to approach them.

Adventurer's Tip: Petrification can be cured by smearing the afflicted person all over with blood, preferably that of a close relative.

The Gorgons (from gorgos, *meaning "dreadful") were three sisters of Greek mythology: Euryale, Stheno, and Medusa. They were minor sea goddesses, with Medusa being the most beautiful and bearing golden hair. After being raped in Athena's temple by Poseidon, Athena punished Medusa by turning her and her sisters into hideous monsters and transforming her hair into snakes. Some myths change this to Athena transforming the Gorgons not to punish them, but to protect them from the unwanted desires of lustful men.*

115

Griffin

a.k.a. Gryphon

COMBAT	☀	☀	☀	☼	☼
MAGIC	☼	☼	☼	☼	☼
SMARTS	☀	☼	☼	☼	☼
LOOT	☀	☀	☀	☼	☼
DANGER	☀	☀	☀	☼	☼

A beast said to be king of the animals of both sky and earth. The griffin displays the ferocity of a lion, the aerial prowess of an eagle, and the majesty of both. They make their homes in rocky mountains and, like dragons, are fond of collecting gems and precious metals, especially gold. Griffins are not especially intelligent, so their hoarding is more a result of a fascination with shiny objects rather than greed or artistic appreciation. These beasts share their nests with a partner and are so devoted that they won't take a new companion after they die. Though it's not impossible to train a griffin, their willfulness and aggression make it a difficult task. Those who overcome those hurdles find themselves the owners of excellent war beasts.

Adventurer's Tip: Do not confuse with similar hybrids, such as the alce (a wingless griffin) or the alphyn (a lion with eagle claws for front legs).

The griffin appears in ancient Greek, Persian, and Egyptian artwork, but became prominent throughout Western art. Due to being part lion (the king of beasts) and part eagle (the king of birds), the griffin made for a powerful heraldic figure, symbolizing strength, nobility, and divinity. Folklorist Adrienne Mayor theorizes that the skeletons of the Protoceratops, a dog-sized beaked dinosaur, were mistaken for griffin bones.

Hag

a.k.a. Cailleach,
Onibaba

COMBAT ☼ ☼ ☆ ☆ ☆
MAGIC ☼ ☼ ☼ ☼ ☆
SMARTS ☼ ☼ ☼ ☼ ☆
LOOT ☼ ☼ ☼ ☆ ☆
DANGER ☼ ☼ ☼ ☆ ☆

An ancient witch, possibly human once but now something else. Hags are very powerful, very secretive, and very, very old. These wizened women often lead isolated lives in inhospitable wastelands, with only familiars and spirits for company. The hag can be a great ally, being able to grant a supplicant a glimpse into the future, provide impossible remedies, or grant power over their foes. However, dealing with a hag can require a price as steep as dealing with a demon or fairy, requiring great sacrifice on the part of those who come to her. She is well aware that only the desperate and foolish seek her out, and she happily takes advantage of them. Her magic is powerful and dark, with her potions and rituals requiring rare and distasteful ingredients.

Adventurer's Tip: If you address a hag with the respect you would give your own grandmother or auntie, maybe she'll decide not to extort too great a payment from you.

Hags, along with witches in general, are arguably a demonization of old women, physically feeble but possessing a store of knowledge gathered over the decades. In myths and fairy tales, the hag could be an ally or enemy, but was always depicted as a withered old woman to be both respected and feared. Among the most famous hags in folklore is Baba Yaga, who appears in many Slavic stories. Heroes would often come across her chicken-legged house in the woods and would be able to enter by commanding it to "stand with your back to the forest and your front to me."

Harpy

a.k.a. Areyiai

COMBAT ✺ ✺ ✺ ✧ ✧

MAGIC ✺ ✧ ✧ ✧ ✧

SMARTS ✺ ✺ ✺ ✧ ✧

LOOT ✺ ✺ ✧ ✧ ✧

DANGER ✺ ✺ ✺ ✧ ✧

An agent of punishment, part woman and part bird. Harpies are most often found in forbidding forests and rocky cliffs, and their presence is a sure sign that there's a gate to the Underworld nearby. They work closely with gods and demons, who send the harpies forth to torment any mortal who has displeased them. Harpies delight in this work and are skilled at drawing out the suffering of their quarry before spiriting them away. Harpies will snatch away food and drink, leaving their victim on the edge of starvation; they'll claw them to ribbons whilst avoiding their vital organs; finally, they'll whisk them away through the air, dropping them and catching them again as they go, shrieking and laughing all the while.

Adventurer's Tip: Not to be confused with sirens, who would rather lead mortals to their doom through song than dirty their claws.

> *From the Greek* harpyai, *meaning "snatcher." Also known as the hounds of Zeus, the harpies were the children of the sea-god Thaumas and sisters to Iris, the rainbow. They themselves were wind spirits, dispatched by Zeus to mete out punishment to mortals who disrespected him. The harpies appear in Dante's* Divine Comedy, *where they torture the souls of suicides in Hell. These poor souls are transfigured into trees, whose bark bleeds as they are clawed relentlessly by the bird-women.*

Hecatoncheires

a.k.a. Centimanes,
Hundred-Handed Ones

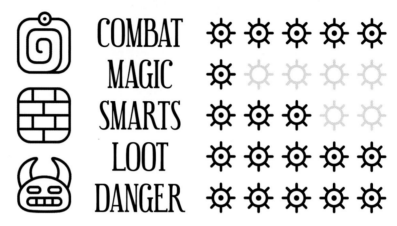

COMBAT	☼	☼	☼	☼	☼
MAGIC	☼	○	○	○	○
SMARTS	☼	☼	☼	○	○
LOOT	☼	☼	☼	☼	☼
DANGER	☼	☼	☼	☼	☼

A creature from primordial times, before the universe could enforce physical limits on its inhabitants. There are a mercifully small number of these monsters in existence. Even the gods fear their great strength, and do their best to keep them locked in inescapable prisons, either under the earth or in other dimensions. When they break their bonds, they ravage the world with earthquakes caused by slamming their hundred arms or with wind storms blown from their fifty mouths. Unlike other many-headed monsters, all the heads of the hecatoncheires work in tandem, making them difficult to fool and almost impossible to sneak up on. Even the best-equipped armies have no hope in besting the monster in combat.

Adventurer's Tip: The gods are your only hope.

From the Greek hekaton *("one hundred") and* kheires *("hands"), they were the three children of the primordial earth goddess Gaia and sky god Ouranus. Thrown into Tartarus by a father who feared their power, they were later released by the god Zeus in his war against the Titans. As a reward, the brothers were returned to the Underworld, not as prisoners but as wardens, guarding the Titans now imprisoned there.*

Hippocampus

a.k.a. Sea Horse

COMBAT ☼ ☼ ☼ ☼ ☼

MAGIC ☼ ☼ ☼ ☼ ☼

SMARTS ☼ ☼ ☼ ☼ ☼

LOOT ☼ ☼ ☼ ☼ ☼

DANGER ☼ ☼ ☼ ☼ ☼

A hybrid beast, like a horse with a fish's tail for hindquarters, that lives in warm ocean waters. It is covered in colorful scales and its mane seems like flowing seaweed or branches of coral. Tamed hippocampi are ridden by mermaids, sea nymphs, and other aquatic spirits, either for sport or in battle. Though ordinarily aquatic, sea gods who need to travel inland may grant their steed back legs or fin-like wings. Even then, the hippocampus is loath to stray too far from the sea, is nervous and skittish on land, and joyously returns to the water. This beast is of animal intellect, so one needn't fear them as inherently cunning or evil. Still, they are swift and strong, standing taller than an ordinary horse.

Adventurer's Tip: Do not confuse the hippocampus with the kelpie, another water horse. The second is as bloodthirsty as the first is shy.

From the Greek hippo *("horse") and* kampos *("sea monster"). This creature is closely associated with Poseidon, god of both the sea and horses. Phoenician coins bear a variant of the hippocampus, displaying fish-tailed horses with wings. Other mythical sea beasts with similar nomenclature include leokampus, taurocampus, and aigikampos (sea lion, sea bull, and sea goat). In modern taxonomy,* Hippocampus *is the genus of seahorses, small fish with elongated horselike heads.*

Hippogriff

a.k.a. Griffin Horse

COMBAT	☀	☀	☀	☼	☼
MAGIC	☼	☼	☼	☼	☼
SMARTS	☀	☼	☼	☼	☼
LOOT	☀	☼	☼	☼	☼
DANGER	☀	☀	☼	☼	☼

A creature said to have first come about from unions between griffins and horses, but given these creatures usually have a predator-prey relationship, it can be safe to assume wizards were somehow involved. Regardless, their offspring have done well enough, and herds of hippogriffs can be found making their homes in rocky mountain ranges. Though weaker than griffins, hippogriffs are swifter than their leonine ancestors and their horse heritage makes them easier to train—though only just. It's possible that pegasi and other varieties of winged horse are themselves descended from the hippogriff, the griffin blood being diluted until the wings are the only avian feature they retain.

Adventurer's Tip: The hooves of a hippogriff are just as dangerous as the claws. Follow the standard horse safety rule: don't stand behind them.

A combination of hippo *("horse") and* gryphos *("griffin"). The earliest suggestion of this beast appears in the first century, in Virgil's* Eclogues, *where a heartbroken shepherd calls for impossible things to happen, including oaks bearing golden apples, wolves fleeing from sheep, and griffins coupling with horses. The first actual appearance by a hippogriff is in Ludovico Ariosto's sixteenth century epic* Orlando Furioso, *where it acts as the steed of the hero Ruggiero.*

127

Homunculus

a.k.a. Clay Servant,
Manikin

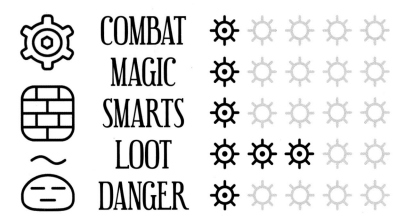

COMBAT ☀ ☼ ☼ ☼ ☼
MAGIC ☀ ☼ ☼ ☼ ☼
SMARTS ☀ ☼ ☼ ☼ ☼
LOOT ☀ ☀ ☀ ☼ ☼
DANGER ☀ ☼ ☼ ☼ ☼

A type of golem, but far smaller and easier to construct. The homunculus is typically created by those spellcasters who would prefer a dim-witted but reliable assistant to an intelligent but potentially treacherous familiar. A figurine is sculpted out of an alchemical mix that includes clay and the creator's own bodily fluids, and is later put through a secret process that grants it life. Homunculi are generally small in stature and have intelligence comparable to that of an infant. The larger a homunculus, the more human fluids are needed to build it, which may result in giving the construct a sense of independence not suitable in a servant. Poorly constructed homunculi rot easily.

Adventurer's Tip: Homunculi can be built with a psychic link to their creators, making them good watchmen and spies.

The homunculus ("little man") has similar roots to the golem: the desire to create artificial life. A number of alchemical recipes involve processes that grotesquely mirror the natural development of a fetus. According to the alchemist Paracelsus, a homunculus can be made by mixing human sperm with horse manure, feeding the resultant growth on human blood, and further incubating it in more manure for forty weeks (about nine months).

Hound, Black

a.k.a. Barghest,
Grim, Shuck

COMBAT ✵ ✵ ✵ ✺ ✺

MAGIC ✵ ✵ ✺ ✺ ✺

SMARTS ✵ ✺ ✺ ✺ ✺

LOOT ✵ ✵ ✺ ✺ ✺

DANGER ✵ ✵ ✵ ✺ ✺

A large dog that haunts crossroads and graveyards, about the size of a calf and covered in dark fur. The black hound is a restless spirit, formed from the collected despair and anger of those who died by execution (whether rightfully or no). A person who reaches out to touch a black hound feels nothing but cold and mist. However, this doesn't mean the hound is some harmless illusion, as when it pounces on its victim, its body suddenly becomes solid and suffocatingly heavy. To encounter a black hound is to know that death is coming soon, as it's able to confer bad luck on those who see it. Still, the bite of the hound is worse, as the painful wounds caused by it do not heal and ooze freely with sepsis.

Adventurer's Tip: Avoid stealing from cemeteries, as black hounds are especially vicious towards graverobbers and body-snatchers.

Legends of black hounds are found in the British Isles, often named after their location (like the Black Dog of Tring, the Black Dog of Newgate, and so on). Depending on the story, the black hound may be a demonic being, a ghostly spirit, or a local guardian. A similar creature, the cadejo, exists in Central American folklore. The black cadejo is an evil dog that attacks travellers or encourages them to perform evil deeds. This beast has his good counterpart in the white cadejo, which protects travellers and drunks from harm.

Hound, Elven

a.k.a. Cù Sìth,
Cŵn Annwn

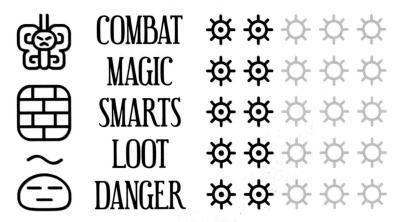

COMBAT ✺✺☼☼☼

MAGIC ✺✺☼☼☼

SMARTS ✺✺☼☼☼

LOOT ✺✺☼☼☼

DANGER ✺✺☼☼☼

A pale-furred dog with green or red markings and a companion to the fairies, serving as guardians, hunting hounds, and mounts. One of this animal's most curious aspects is its voice, which sounds more like a honk than a bark and is louder when heard at a distance than when heard nearby. Sometimes the Good People will allow a mortal to own an elven hound. For years, the hound will do nothing, merely laying about in an entirely useless manner, sometimes causing their frustrated owner to get rid of them. However, patience with these animals wins out; the elven hound will perform one life-saving task for their mortal, after which point they will disappear, returning to the fairy realm.

Adventurer's Tip: All dogs are good at detecting invisible supernatural forces, but elven hounds actually stand a chance in a fight.

This is a creature of Celtic myth, reappearing in Welsh, Scottish, and Irish folklore. They're often interchangeable with hell hounds, as both were used in the Wild Hunt, a myth where magical beings hunt down the souls of the recently deceased. Where a hunt involving the Devil inevitably led to Hell, hunts involving fairies led to the Otherworld, a realm that could either be an eternity of drudgery or an everlasting paradise. Corgis are said to be descended from a fairy breed, with their marking being made by the riding harnesses they were made to wear.

Hound, Hell

a.k.a. Dandy Dog,
Yeth Hound

COMBAT	☼ ☼ ☼ ☼ ☼	
MAGIC	☼ ☼ ☼ ☼ ☼	
SMARTS	☼ ☼ ☼ ☼ ☼	
LOOT	☼ ☼ ☼ ☼ ☼	
DANGER	☼ ☼ ☼ ☼ ☼	

These are the monstrous canine slaves of the infernal legions. They are made from the souls of the damned, twisted and malformed, sometimes having too many of this body part and too few of another. The largest and most attentive of these beasts guard the gates of the Underworld, while the rest are allowed to run rampant within Hell, tearing apart the souls of the dead. Demons sometimes organize sorties into the mortal world, riding nightmares and followed by packs of baying hell hounds, searching for souls to drag into Hell. As with earthly hounds, hell hounds are excellent trackers but their stealth leaves something to be desired; the light from their fiery eyes and mouths along with the rattling of their chains give them away in the darkness.

Adventurer's Tip: Like most demons and the undead, sunlight and holy ground is anathema to them. If chased, run to the nearest consecrated temple.

Since the dog is a useful companion to people, deities and supernatural forces similarly have their own canine attendants. The archetypal hell hound in the West is Cerberus of Greek mythology, who was tasked with guarding the gates of Hades. He was said to have up to a thousand heads, the main three being dog heads and the rest belonging to snakes which covered his body. Though generally a good guardian, Cerberus was bested by the heroes Hercules and Orpheus.

Hydra

a.k.a. Many-Headed Serpent

COMBAT ✪ ✪ ✪ ✪ ✧

MAGIC ✪ ✪ ✧ ✧ ✧

SMARTS ✪ ✧ ✧ ✧ ✧

LOOT ✪ ✪ ✪ ✧ ✧

DANGER ✪ ✪ ✪ ✪ ✧

A serpent living in fetid swamps, sporting many heads. Even if the area the hydra lives in was once an idyllic stream or lake, it won't be long before the monster's poisonous breath blights the surrounding vegetation and taints the water. Though other multi-headed dragons exist, the hydra's claim to fame is its regenerative abilities. Severing a head causes two more to spring from the bloody stump, eventually resulting in an overwhelming mass of snapping heads. One of the hydra's heads is immortal, continuing to fight when removed and, if given enough space and time, it will regrow its body, forming a new hydra. Hydra bile is a necrotic poison and wounds exposed to it will not heal.

Adventurer's Tip: The regenerative abilities of many monsters can be counteracted with fire or acid. Once a wound has been cauterized, the hydra's body cannot regrow any missing parts.

Multi-headed serpents and dragons are a recurring trope in myth and legend, but only the Greek Lernaean Hydra could regenerate its heads. Killing the monster was the second of the demigod Hercules' twelve tasks and, assisted by Iolaus, he was able to defeat it, trapping the immortal head under a rock. Chudo Yudo of Russian folklore is a similar beast, being a lake-dwelling dragon with multiple heads. At first three-headed, it would retreat to the water after fighting the hero, but return the following day with six, then nine, and finally twelve heads.

Jiangshi

a.k.a. Hopping Vampire

COMBAT	☀ ☼ ☼ ☼ ☼
MAGIC	☀ ☀ ☼ ☼ ☼
SMARTS	☀ ☼ ☼ ☼ ☼
LOOT	☀ ☀ ☼ ☼ ☼
DANGER	☀ ☀ ☀ ☼ ☼

A soul-eating ghoul, its movement thankfully restricted by a combination of funerary bindings and rigor mortis. Unable to move except by graceless shuffling or hopping, the typical jiangshi is easy to outrun provided you see it coming. This vampiric monster doesn't subsist on blood or flesh, instead draining the invisible spiritual energy of living things. Though blind, deaf, and not terribly intelligent, it can pinpoint a victim's location by sensing their breath. The jiangshi then tries to get close to its target, immobilizing them with its claws if possible, and sucks out their life energy by breathing on them. The more energy a jiangshi absorbs, the better it can move, and some have been observed to cross fifty feet with a single hop.

Adventurer's Tip: Many undead can't see the living and rely on sensing their life energy. Breathing reveals life energy, so a good way to avoid the attention of ghosts is to hold your breath while they're nearby.

A monster of Chinese folklore, literally translating to "stiff corpse." Some stories say that when Chinese laborers or soldiers died far from home, priests would transport the bodies back, enchanting the corpse so it would hop along behind them. A number of comedic Hong Kong films have been made about this monster, such as Encounters of the Spooky Kind *(1980) and* Mr. Vampire *(1985). The pocong of Indonesia and Malaysia is a similar undead spirit, this particular monster being trapped in a traditional burial shroud.*

139

Kaibyo

a.k.a. Bakeneko,
Cat Sith

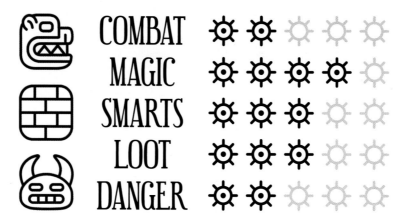

COMBAT ☼ ☼ ☼ ☼ ☼
MAGIC ☼ ☼ ☼ ☼ ☼
SMARTS ☼ ☼ ☼ ☼ ☼
LOOT ☼ ☼ ☼ ☼ ☼
DANGER ☼ ☼ ☼ ☼ ☼

A creature that was once an ordinary house cat, but has somehow attained dangerous supernatural powers. The way a cat can become a kaibyo varies, be it consuming human flesh, being possessed by spirits, receiving abuse from its owners, or attaining a certain age. These cat spirits are able to walk on their hind legs, speak, shapeshift, and cast necromantic spells. If it was treated well when a normal cat, the kaibyo is merely mischievous, tricking mortals with poltergeist-like antics. Those who were treated poorly are especially dangerous and vengeful, killing their masters the first chance they get, then transforming into them to take their place. Some kaibyo can create undead by capturing the soul as it leaves a dying body, allowing the cat to control the corpse.

Adventurer's Tip: A kaibyo in human form cannot suppress its feline instincts, and can't help chasing after mice or birds or overindulging in fish.

> *Kaibyo ("ghostly cat") is a Japanese umbrella term for supernatural felines, which include the kasha (a fiery corpse-thief), nekomata (a split-tailed necromancer), and bakeneko (a shapeshifter). The belief that a cat's long tail was the source of its evil powers likely led to the popularity of the Japanese Bobtail, a cat breed with a mutation that causes a short, rabbit-like tail. Cats are not free from superstition in the West, as they're often associated with witches and are said to be able to suck out souls by lying on sleeping people's chests.*

141

Kappa

a.k.a. River Child

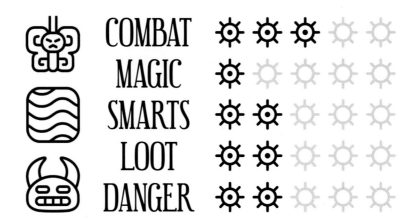

COMBAT ☼ ☼ ☼ ☆ ☆

MAGIC ☼ ☆ ☆ ☆ ☆

SMARTS ☼ ☼ ☆ ☆ ☆

LOOT ☼ ☼ ☆ ☆ ☆

DANGER ☼ ☼ ☆ ☆ ☆

A small creature that looks like a mix of monkey, turtle, waterfowl, and frog. Kappas live in rivers and ponds—especially those with a surface layer of scum to hide under—popping up to insult and harass any people who pass nearby. Though child-sized, these water goblins are strong, expert wrestlers, frequently forcing people and animals several times bigger than them into the water to drown. Though they enjoy eating human organs, their favorite food is fermented vegetables (especially cucumbers) and will gladly stop their harassment if bribed with these foodstuffs. The kappa's most notable feature is the shallow, dish-like depression on top of their head, which is filled with water. Should the water spill, the monster may be drained of its strength, paralyzed, or even die.

Adventurer's Tip: Despite delighting in rude behavior and coarse language, kappas can't resist bowing back to those who bow to them, causing the water to spill out of their heads and leave them weakened.

A very popular Japanese creature blamed for drownings and often used as a bogeyman to frighten children away from dangerous waterways. Though today it's often depicted as a mischievous creature, the kappa could be an outright murderer and rapist in old tales. It would kill by reaching up its victim's anus to tear out their liver or extract their shirikodama—an onion-shaped ball found in the rectum, said to be the embodiment of the human soul.

Kelpie

a.k.a. Brook Horse

COMBAT ☼ ☼ ☼ ☼ ☼

MAGIC ☼ ☼ ☼ ☼ ☼

SMARTS ☼ ☼ ☼ ☼ ☼

LOOT ☼ ☼ ☼ ☼ ☼

DANGER ☼ ☼ ☼ ☼ ☼

A beautiful flesh-eating horse that lives in bodies of fresh water. The kelpie's coat is pale (though maybe a little mud-spattered), its eyes alert and intelligent, and its build graceful. It stands by rivers and lakes and looks like a perfectly tame horse, maybe an escapee from some nearby noble's stables. It would be a shame *not* to ride it. Once on the willing "horse," the rider finds themselves stuck to its back, which grotesquely extends to fit more passengers. Somehow, other potential victims don't seem to notice this horrible deformation, nor can they hear the warnings of the kelpie's prisoners. A kelpie can trap up to a dozen people in this manner, which it drowns and eats after galloping into the water.

Adventurer's Tip: Do not confuse the kelpie with the sea-dwelling hippocampus, a comparatively docile beast.

This is a creature of Celtic folklore, possibly imported by Norse settlers who have a similar creature called the bäckahäst. Most kelpie legends involve them abducting travellers, though the Scottish legend of the Laird of Morphie is different. In this story, a nobleman enslaves a kelpie by stealing its magic bridle and forces it to build a castle. When the humiliated, half-starved kelpie is released, it curses the Morphie bloodline, causing the family to die out and the castle to fall to ruin.

Kitsune

a.k.a. Fox Spirit

COMBAT ☼ ☼ ☼ ☼ ☼

MAGIC ☼ ☼ ☼ ☼ ☼

SMARTS ☼ ☼ ☼ ☼ ☼

LOOT ☼ ☼ ☼ ☼ ☼

DANGER ☼ ☼ ☼ ☼ ☼

An intelligent, magical fox that grows extra tails as it ages. Kitsune start out as ordinary animals, albeit ones of unusual cunning. As they age, they gain the power of speech and magic, being able to cast illusions, shapeshift, enchant, and possess people to induce sickness. The number of tails is indicative of its magical prowess, with nine-tailed foxes being the oldest and most powerful. Kitsune live as family groups in dens under shrubbery or haystacks, and sometimes even take on human form to rent luxurious gardens from landlords. When they bring human visitors to their homes, they use illusions to make their dens looks like lavish palaces. Kitsune disguises are imperfect (they often forget to change the tail), and they cast fox-shaped shadows and reflections.

Adventurer's Tip: Dogs hate foxes and can sniff out a kitsune in any shape. Be suspicious of visitors who insist all dogs be locked away.

Magical foxes are frequent characters in East Asian folktales. While some are treated as good omens, such as the white foxes of the Japanese rice god Inari, most are either mischievous or evil. Chinese foxes are especially succubuslike, making their victims overindulge in sex, which kills them by throwing off their balance of Yin and Yang. Though the West doesn't have much in the way of magical foxes, they're still depicted as clever tricksters in folktales, frequently getting the best of others, especially wolves and hunters.

Kraken

a.k.a. Architeuthis,
Giant Squid

COMBAT	☼	☼	☼	☼	☼
MAGIC					
SMARTS	☼				
LOOT	☼	☼	☼		
DANGER	☼	☼	☼	☼	

A tentacled sea creature of massive size, much bigger than a whale. The kraken enjoys dozing on the surface of the ocean, basking in the sun, lazily eating the fish that swim in its shadow. Many are those sailors who, after long weeks on a pitiless, never-ending voyage, mistake the floating beast's bulk for dry land. When the kraken feels the sailors crawling on its body, starting campfires and driving tent spikes into its flesh, it quickly works up into a rage. The sea monster wraps its tentacles around the offending ship, easily crushing it to matchsticks. As the kraken sinks back to the cold depths of the ocean, its huge body creates a whirlpool, dragging in any poor unfortunates who thought to escape by swimming or using lifeboats.

Adventurer's Tip: Always set out a small expedition to examine islands that don't appear on your map. If the "ground" is unusually slimy and warm, get back on your boat and sail away.

Legends of the kraken tell of it living in the waters around Greenland, Iceland, and Norway. Early descriptions mostly refer to its great size and are vague as to whether it was a fish, whale, crab, or mollusk. The association with squid and octopi was sealed in 1802, when French naturalist Pierre Denys de Montfort published a book, Histoire Naturelle Générale et Particulière des Mollusques, *featuring the now-famous illustration of a giant octopus attacking a ship. Though giant squids exist, they live deep in the ocean and don't interact much with boats.*

149

Lamia

a.k.a. Child-Eater,
Laestrygonian

COMBAT ✹ ✹ ✹ ✧ ✧
MAGIC ✹ ✹ ✧ ✧ ✧
SMARTS ✹ ✹ ✹ ✧ ✧
LOOT ✹ ✹ ✧ ✧ ✧
DANGER ✹ ✹ ✹ ✧ ✧

A woman who killed her child, transformed into an evil spirit by grief, anger, and shame. Lamias have two forms: that of a normal woman, her face contorted with grief and anguish; and a monstrous one, half woman, half-beast. When in beastly shape, the lower body of a lamia is snakelike or shaped like a scaled lion, and her weeping human face has no eyelids. Lamias mainly appear at night or in dark places, near where they committed their original crime, and wander around weeping and calling for their lost child. They will kidnap any child they come across, partially to fill a void in their hearts, but also to spite successful mothers. Lamias cannot suppress their murderous urges, killing and eating the stolen infant and starting their grief anew.

Adventurer's Tip: There are already many reasons why children shouldn't be allowed to go outside without supervision.

> *Greek myth's Lamia was a princess of Libya, who had the misfortune of attracting the affections of Zeus and bearing his children. Hera, Zeus' wife, forced Lamia to eat them, driving the princess mad and transforming her into a monster. The child-eating woman is a common bogeyman, a famous example being Mexico's La Llorona ("the crying woman"). La Llorona is the ghost of a woman denied entrance to Heaven after she drowned her sons, and she now wanders the earth, kidnapping and drowning children to try to trick her way through the pearly gates.*

Leviathan

a.k.a. The Great Whale

COMBAT	☼	☼	☼	☼	☼
MAGIC	☼	☼			
SMARTS	☼				
LOOT	☼	☼	☼	☼	
DANGER	☼	☼	☼	☼	☼

The greatest of all the sea beasts, an aquatic monster from primordial times. All waterborne animals are but pale reflections of the Leviathan. It exists both in this world and outside it, as no earthly ocean is big enough to contain it. Its hide is impenetrable to all weapons, and its belly is covered with rough scales. The blood of the Leviathan runs so hot than the water boils around it as it swims, raising tornadoes and hot mists. Tidal waves are formed with each stroke of its fins and the earth shakes when it snores as it sleeps on the ocean floor. Only the gods will slay the Leviathan, and only for the banquet before the end of the Universe, which will be attended by all those who have ever lived.

Adventurer's Tip: No ship stands a chance against the great Leviathan, so large that the greatest dreadnought is as krill to it, to be eaten without a thought.

A creature from Abrahamic mythology, often mentioned alongside the land-beast Behemoth and the bird-griffin Ziz. Many legends have giant sea creatures that cause tidal waves and earthquakes; the Ōnamazu of Japanese myth is a giant catfish trapped under a rock by the gods, causing tremors as he struggles. The stories of giant fish may be inspired by whales, who seem to breathe smoke when they blow water from their spouts. Indeed, "leviathan" is the Modern Hebrew word for "whale."

Lich

a.k.a. Undead Wizard

COMBAT	☀	☼	☼	☼	☼
MAGIC	☀	☀	☀	☀	☼
SMARTS	☀	☀	☀	☀	☼
LOOT	☀	☀	☀	☀	☼
DANGER	☀	☀	☀	☀	☼

A very powerful wizard that has found a way to cheat death at the expense of his soul. Many are spellcasters and alchemists who seek a way to conquer death, spending decades in this futile pursuit. Certain dark spells allow one to trap one's own soul in a special container, placing it beyond the reach of psychopomps, turning the spellcaster into a lich. The body, mind, and soul should exist as a single unit, however, and this unnatural separation has terrible consequences. Though a lich will not die, its body will twist and decay, and while the mind remains sharp, it soon develops delusions of divine grandeur. Many liches amass armies of monsters, demons, and undead minions, seeking to take over nations and place themselves as god-kings.

Adventurer's Tip: The special containers liches keep their souls in are called phylacteries. As destroying the phylactery kills the lich, these undead wizards keep them well hidden and guarded.

Derived from leiche, *an archaic Germanic word for "corpse," this term was used by early twentieth century fantasy authors to describe evil sorcerers who conquered death through magic, and has since become an archetypal villain in the genre. Koschei the Deathless, a villain of Slavic folklore, could be called a lich. He could only be killed by destroying his soul, which was hidden in a needle, which was in an egg, which was in a duck, which was in a hare, which was locked in an iron chest, which was buried under a tree on a remote island.*

Lightning Spirit

a.k.a. Electric Elemental,
Storm Spirit

COMBAT	☀	☀	☼	☼	☼
MAGIC	☀	☀	☀	☼	☼
SMARTS	☀	☀	☼	☼	☼
LOOT	☀	☀	☀	☼	☼
DANGER	☀	☀	☼	☼	☼

A spirit related to air and fire elementals, sometimes called a quasi-elemental. Though lightning spirits generally live in the clouds, some of them have been known to manifest on land. This is likely caused by alchemists toying with certain acids and metals, creating a magical energy which can lead to the spontaneous manifestation of these creatures. The lightning spirit is cheerful, excitable, and very speedy, and their bodies produce electrical discharges, the power of which corresponds to their size. Smaller spirits only emit sparks, but large ones produce blinding arcs of sizzling light and rolls of thunderous sound. These creatures can be trapped in special glass or clay containers and should not be allowed near metal or water.

Adventurer's Tip: Lightning spirits can move through metal, making most armor and weapons useless against them. In fact, the metal makes their shocks all the more deadly.

Since religion is tied to human beings trying to understand and explain natural phenomena, most pantheons have gods and spirits who control storms. Eastern storm gods are often depicted holding a vajra, a ribbed, two-headed club representing lightning. Though modern fantasy sometimes treats electricity or lightning as an element, it doesn't appear in the Eastern or Classical elemental charts (these containing ether, air, earth, fire, qi, metal, void, water, and wood).

Living Toy

a.k.a. Living Doll

COMBAT ☀ ☼ ☼ ☼ ☼
MAGIC ☀ ☼ ☼ ☼ ☼
SMARTS ☀ ☀ ☼ ☼ ☼
LOOT ☀ ☀ ☼ ☼ ☼
DANGER ☀ ☼ ☼ ☼ ☼

A child's plaything, somehow having attained sentience. Toys that share physical features with people or animals are especially prone to coming to life, as the attention and personalities children assign to these objects can cause a soul to spontaneously coalesce within it. Spellcasters who specialize in golem-building find this kind of magic frustrating, unpredictable, and unrefined, and are resentful of the children who accidentally channel it, when it takes them years of study to achieve the same result. The living toy's main ambition and joy is to please its owner, as they're dependent on their love and may become lifeless if forgotten or abandoned. Sometimes toys seek the friendship of a new child to keep themselves alive. Ill-treated toys have been known to turn vengeful.

Adventurer's Tip: You never know if a toy is alive or not, since they imitate lifelessness when they're not in the presence of their child.

A common trope in children's media. Sometimes the toy is brought to life by magic, such as with the various versions of puppet-boy Pinocchio, who was made from magical wood in the original story and brought to life by a fairy in the Disney film. Often the toys have been secretly sentient all along, as seen in countless children's stories from the eighteenth century onwards. Pixar's Toy Story *series is probably the most famous of this last type and frequently deals with themes of love, jealousy, mortality, and abandonment.*

Manticore

a.k.a. Baricos,
Mantyger

COMBAT ☼ ☼ ☼ ☼ ☼

MAGIC ☼ ☼ ☼ ☼ ☼

SMARTS ☼ ☼ ☼ ☼ ☼

LOOT ☼ ☼ ☼ ☼ ☼

DANGER ☼ ☼ ☼ ☼ ☼

A beast with a red leonine body, the face of a man, and a long spiny tail. While winged manticores exist, these are thankfully rare. Despite boasting sharp claws and teeth, the manticore's primary weapon is its tail, which is covered in long poisonous quills. When the manticore whips its tail, these spikes are cast forth at great speed, falling upon their target like a volley of arrows. Spent quills regrow in a few hours, allowing the monster to make regular use of this attack. This animal is carnivorous and especially fond of human flesh, and has been known to toy with its prey before killing it. Its three rows of teeth allow it to eat its victims whole, bones and all, leaving no more than a few drops of blood behind.

Adventurer's Tip: Encourage the manticore to use up its spikes on a decoy. It'll still be dangerous, but at least that's one less weapon at its disposal.

> *The manticore was said to live in India, Persia, or Ethiopia, countries often used interchangeably in old texts. Called martikhora in Old Iranian, the word translates to "man-eater," from* martiya *("man") and* khvara *("eater"). The second century Greek traveller Pausanias thought the beast was a version of the tiger, turned into a monster by peasants' imaginations, while the sixteenth century cleric Edward Topsell classified it among hyena-related beasts. In modern taxonomy, the* Manticoras, *a genus of beetle, is named after this monster.*

Merfolk

a.k.a. Mermaid,
Ningyo

COMBAT	☀ ☀ ☼ ☼ ☼
MAGIC	☀ ☼ ☼ ☼ ☼
SMARTS	☀ ☀ ☀ ☼ ☼
LOOT	☀ ☀ ☼ ☼ ☼
DANGER	☀ ☼ ☼ ☼ ☼

An aquatic race, having a humanoid top half and a fish tail instead of legs. Merfolk make their homes in lakes and the sea, and may be sighted in surrounding rivers and estuaries. They are a relatively friendly people, rarely aggressive and often playful with sailors and fishermen. Said playfulness can lead to tragedy, as merfolk often forget about their terrestrial companions' inability to breathe underwater, resulting in accidental drownings. The female of the species is said to be especially attractive and to possess a beautiful voice. Courtships between merfolk and humans are possible, but only with magical aid, and children born of this union will have an unusual fascination with water. The tears of merfolk are thick, solidifying into glass or gemstones soon after being shed.

Adventurer's Tip: It's difficult to tell apart merfolk from water nymphs, but all of them can love you, drown you, or both.

> *Merpeople are common throughout the world, with the earliest appearance being in an Assyrian legend. The goddess Atargatis fell in love with a human and later threw herself in a lake in shame. The water turned her bottom half into a fish's tail, but was unable to fully hide her beauty, leaving her top half human. The belief in mermaids persists today with occasional sightings, photographs, or dead examples being reported as proof. Mermaid "corpses" are often just desiccated manta rays or taxidermy combining monkey and fish parts.*

Mimic

a.k.a. Trick Treasure

COMBAT ☼ ☼ ☼ ☼ ☼
MAGIC ☼ ☼ ☼ ☼ ☼
SMARTS ☼ ☼ ☼ ☼ ☼
LOOT ☼ ☼ ☼ ☼ ☼
DANGER ☼ ☼ ☼ ☼ ☼

A creature with the ability to alter its shape and texture to perfectly imitate any inanimate object. The mimic is primarily an ambush predator, transforming its body into anything its chosen prey is most likely to approach. Mimics don't speak, making it difficult to gauge their intelligence, but their seeming pleasure at tricking humans suggests they're smarter than ordinary animals. The typical dungeon-dwelling mimic often disguises itself as a chest filled with gold and gems. Once an adventurer reaches in to grab the alluring treasure, the edges of the lid sprout fangs and shut on the adventurer's arm. Mimics are loath to imitate other creatures; while their skill at visual imitation is great, their ability to affect the behavior and movement of living things is sorely lacking.

Adventurer's Tip: A long stick is an indispensable tool in the adventurer's survival kit, as it can be used to check for illusions, trigger traps, and annoy mimics into revealing themselves.

The mimic makes an early appearance in the first Dungeons & Dragons *manuals, but is now a staple monster in both tabletop and video games, such as the gangly, chest-headed mimics of the* Dark Souls *series. A number of cephalopods have astounding control over their chromatophores (pigment-containing cells in the skin), allowing them to change their color and texture, and they use this ability to perfectly blend in against rocks, seaweed, and coral. Some may also rearrange their tentacles to look like other sea creatures, such as lionfish and sea snakes.*

Minotaur

a.k.a. Bull-Headed Man

COMBAT ✸ ✸ ✸ ☼ ☼
MAGIC ✸ ☼ ☼ ☼ ☼
SMARTS ✸ ✸ ✸ ☼ ☼
LOOT ✸ ✸ ☼ ☼ ☼
DANGER ✸ ✸ ✸ ☼ ☼

A brutish creature, having the body of a large, muscular man and the head of a bull. Minotaurs are dim-witted, driven by boundless rage. Said rage aids them in combat, as it will mount with every wound, numbing the pain and increasing their martial fervor. Minotaurs can be made to wield weapons and shields, but are too simple-minded to learn any tactic more complex than running forward and smashing. These monsters are most frequently employed as brute muscle, either being trapped in halls to guard against intruders or being sent out to chase down a target. They can be born from humans as a form of divine (or infernal) intervention, quickly maturing from a baby into a huge monster. Despite their bovine heads, minotaurs are flesh-eaters.

Adventurer's Tip: The minotaur can be worked up into a literal blind rage, making it so angry that it can't focus on its target. Make your escape while the monster smashes furniture and walls.

The Minotaur is a unique creature of Greek myth, literally "The Bull of Minos." It was born from King Minos' wife Pasiphae and a magic bull, and was trapped in a labyrinth and fed prisoners. Though generally called the Minotaur, the creature's given name is Asterion. Similar creatures feature in legends from other nations. Though Hindu texts describe the demon Mahishasura as a shapeshifter, he is often depicted as a buffalo or buffalo-headed man. The gates of the Chinese Underworld are guarded by the demon Ox-Head and his companion, Horse-Face.

Mummy

a.k.a. Tomb King

COMBAT	✸ ✸ ✩ ✩ ✩
MAGIC	✸ ✸ ✸ ✩ ✩
SMARTS	✸ ✸ ✸ ✩ ✩
LOOT	✸ ✸ ✸ ✸ ✩
DANGER	✸ ✸ ✸ ✩ ✩

A desiccated body, prepared in such a way as to allow the soul to return. While superficially similar to liches, the magic that grants mummies immortality is attained with the consent of death gods. Members of the royal or religious classes are most likely to be transformed into mummies and are kept in a dormant state in order to extend their rule or to rise at a later date to aid their descendants. The ruin of death is delayed by perfumed unguents on the body and charms attached to funerary wrappings. After time eventually defeats their ancient empires, the mummy is content to sleep for eternity. Disturbing its opulent tomb may cause the mummy to rise in a rage, relentlessly stalking the trespasser until it revenges itself.

Adventurer's Tip: Return stolen treasures immediately.

> *Mummies are called such because of mummia, the mix of waxes and herbs used to prepare the corpse for burial. The legend of the mummy's curse gained traction in the twentieth century, after a number of unlucky incidents involving the discoverers of Tutankhamun's tomb. Considering the long history of exploitation of mummies by the West, it's surprising any curses didn't come into effect sooner. Stolen mummies had long been ground up into medicine and paint, and from the eighteenth century onwards were purchased as fashionable souvenirs by wealthy European travellers and made the subjects of unwrapping parties.*

169

Mushroomfolk

COMBAT ☼ ☼ ✧ ✧ ✧
MAGIC ☼ ✧ ✧ ✧ ✧
SMARTS ☼ ☼ ✧ ✧ ✧
LOOT ☼ ☼ ✧ ✧ ✧
DANGER ☼ ☼ ✧ ✧ ✧

A sentient mushroom, most often sighted in the darker regions of the forest, ponderously shambling among the trees and moss. Famously shy, mushroomfolk stay far from the bustle of human civilization, serving as stoic watchers over their hallowed groves. Whilst their bodies may seem weak and pallid, they are famously resilient, as their skin is tough and fibrous, easily trapping weapons. Though the matter that makes up the core of their bodies is soft and spongy, cutting into it doesn't seem to cause the mushroomfolk much pain. Larger specimens will not hesitate to gang together to protect their young and weak from outsiders. Especially dangerous are the poisonous spores they can loosen from their caps, which can permanently damage the throat and lungs.

Adventurer's Tip: When traveling through certain forests, cover your mouth with a cloth or specialized mask to filter spore-laden air.

The straight stem and broad cap of many mushrooms make them especially easy to anthropomorphize into little hat-wearing men. The mushroom-man appears in all sorts of media, from illustrations to video games. The Mushroom Kingdom from the Mario *series of games is inhabited by mushroom people, the most famous of which is Toad, friend and assistant to Princess Peach. Since fungi are also associated with rot and death, dangerous mushroom-men feature heavily in the Japanese film* Matango *and the video game* The Last of Us.

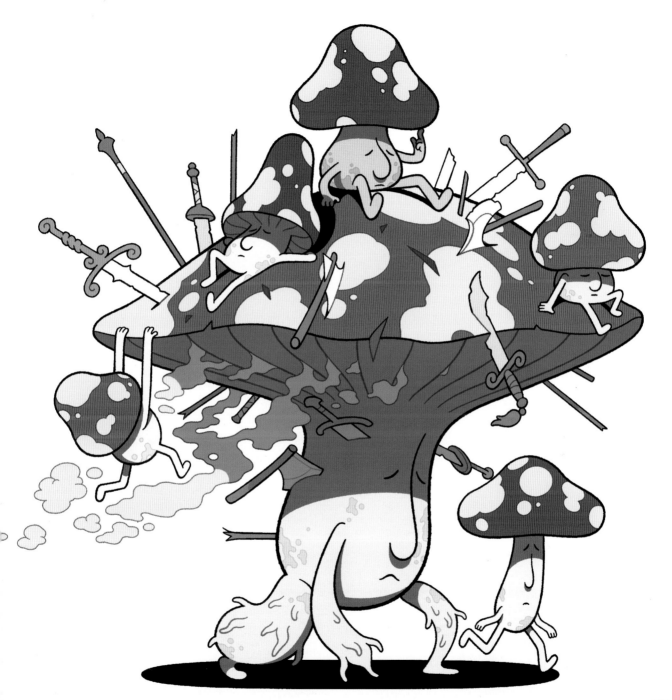

Naga

a.k.a. Naag

COMBAT	✵ ✵ ✵ ☼ ☼	
MAGIC	✵ ✵ ✵ ☼ ☼	
SMARTS	✵ ✵ ✵ ☼ ☼	
LOOT	✵ ✵ ☼ ☼ ☼	
DANGER	✵ ✵ ✵ ☼ ☼	

A semi-divine race of serpents closely related to dragons, nagas appear as great snakes sometimes bearing either human heads or upper bodies. The most powerful among the naga possess multiple heads, and they rule their people from underground or underwater castles lavishly decorated with gold and jewels. Nagas may be good or evil, but they should always be considered dangerous due to their venomous fangs and magical powers. Ordinary snakes may become nagas by abstaining from biting living creatures for a century and attaining enlightenment. Nagas hold a special loathing for birds, as their people are locked in perpetual combat with the garuda, a race of bird-people.

Adventurer's Tip: It can be difficult to tell whether a snake is an ordinary animal or some divine/demonic being, so it's best to just leave them be.

> *A primarily Southeast Asian creature, appearing in Taoic and Dharmic religions, very similar (sometimes identical) to Asian dragons. Though they can be evil figures, many naga kings ally themselves with the gods, such as Sesha, the thousand-headed naga who holds the universe on its head. Divine serpents are rare in the West, though the city of Athens was supposedly founded by Cecrops I, who was born spontaneously from the earth and had the upper half of a man and the lower half of a snake.*

Nightmare

a.k.a. Hell Horse

COMBAT	✸ ✸ ✸ ✧ ✧	
MAGIC	✸ ✸ ✸ ✧ ✧	
SMARTS	✸ ✸ ✧ ✧ ✧	
LOOT	✸ ✸ ✸ ✧ ✧	
DANGER	✸ ✸ ✸ ✧ ✧	

A massive black or flame-colored horse used as a mount or beast of burden by demons and other evil creatures. Dark smoke pours from the nightmare's nostrils and sparks fly as it strikes the ground, leaving behind flaming hoofprints. These creatures are impossible to tame by ordinary mortals without magical aid, as they are happy to buck off and trample any would-be riders. Enchanted bridles and harnesses force them into obedience, but must be kept on at all times lest the horse try to escape. Nightmares are supernaturally swift and can move though different realms, including the lands of death and sleep. Wild nightmares that roam the mortal world can cause bad dreams when they pass near human habitations.

Adventurer's Tip: Some demon kings keep their nightmares bound to rings, summoning them by turning the ring three times. A mortal possessing this ring has dominion over its bound nightmare.

The original nightmare is not a horse, but in fact a Germanic goblin (simply called a mare), one of many folkloric creatures who sit on the chests of sleepers to give them bad dreams. The equine nightmare is a pun, a combination of the English word "mare" (a female horse) and the evil associated with the night and bad dreams. Henry Fuseli's The Nightmare *painting shows both the goblin and horse. A similar creature could be the pooka of the British Isles, a mischievous fairy spirit, often depicted as a horse, but could also appear as a cow, dog, bird, or other animal.*

Nixie

a.k.a. Neck,
Water Sprite

COMBAT	☀	☆	☆	☆	☆
MAGIC	☀	☀	☆	☆	☆
SMARTS	☀	☀	☀	☆	☆
LOOT	☀	☀	☆	☆	☆
DANGER	☀	☀	☆	☆	☆

A minor spirit of freshwater places, known for their beautiful voices and mastery of stringed instruments. Nixies are generally lonesome creatures and crave entertainment, with especially nasty ones enjoying the game of luring and killing music-lovers. They sit near their ponds, drawing people close with beautiful songs and compelling them to drown in their waters. Nixies may promise a person safe passage, an abundant catch of fish, or the secret of their music, often in exchange for some dear sacrifice. In their true form, nixies have greenish, frog-like skin, messy hair, and sharp teeth; they can take on human shape, though their clothes are perpetually wet at the edges, dripping scummy water.

Adventurer's Tip: To protect yourself from a nixie, carry a piece of iron. Even something as small as a needle can protect you from the nixie's charming song.

A creature of Germanic and Scandinavian folklore, similar to water nymphs. While nymphs are ubiquitously female, nixies, necks, and the like could be of either sex. Some stories also describe this creature with attributes similar to that of the kelpie, and are able to take on the shape of a horse. In one of Grimm's fairy tales, a destitute miller enters into a pact with a nixie that lives in his millpond, where she offers him wealth in exchange for the creature that was just born in his house. The man agrees, not realizing he's just promised to hand over his newborn son.

Nymph, River

a.k.a. Naiad,
Rusalka

COMBAT	☀	☆	☆	☆	☆
MAGIC	☀	☀	☀	☆	☆
SMARTS	☀	☀	☀	☆	☆
LOOT	☀	☀	☀	☆	☆
DANGER	☀	☀	☆	☆	☆

A female spirit who protects springs, lakes, and other freshwater places. The river nymph is especially known for her luminous beauty and fickle nature. River nymphs enjoy resting on the rocks around their homes, singing and combing their hair, with passersby who see them becoming instantly smitten. Depending on how she feels, the nymph may reciprocate the attention, disappear into the water, or draw the suitor in, drowning them in her cold embrace. A river nymph generally keeps her lower half submerged to hide her tail and feet, which would reveal her as a fairy rather than a mortal woman. Enraged nymphs have been known to make their rivers overflow, submerging nearby towns and drowning everyone there.

Adventurer's Tip: Cover your eyes when speaking to a river nymph to avoid being hypnotized by them.

The classical freshwater nymph comes from Greek mythology, but the importance of water sources mean that many other civilizations have their own water spirits. Sometimes nymphs have animal skins, appearing as birds, seals, or fish when they wear them, and beautiful women when they don't. Mortal men steal and hide these skins, robbing the nymphs of the means to return home and forcing them into marriage. Later, if a man grows careless in hiding this skin, the nymph may be able to retrieve it and escape to the water, taking any children she bore with her.

Nymph, Sea

a.k.a. Haliai,
Jengu

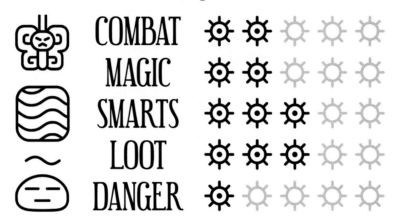

COMBAT	✷ ✷ ✸ ✸ ✸	
MAGIC	✷ ✷ ✸ ✸ ✸	
SMARTS	✷ ✷ ✷ ✸ ✸	
LOOT	✷ ✷ ✷ ✸ ✸	
DANGER	✷ ✸ ✸ ✸ ✸	

Female spirits who protect the sea, often the daughters and proxies of powerful ocean gods. Though sea nymphs are generally peaceful, they can be dangerous if they feel coastal communities and sailors are disrespecting their waters. As punishment, they may cause shipwrecks with tempests or thick mists, call up sea creatures both magical and mundane to attack swimmers, or draw away fish to drive towns to starvation. To appease the sea nymphs, the offending humans must offer them a sacrifice, either animal or human. The nymphs live in undersea palaces built of shell and coral, and their servants are talking fish and other sea beasts. Mortals brought to these kingdoms are somehow able to breathe underwater.

Adventurer's Tip: Helping a beached dolphin or injured turtle may result in the animal telling their fairy masters of your kindness, who in turn may reward you with a treasure the next time you go fishing.

There are many sea nymphs in Greek mythology, being the daughters of numerous sea gods including Triton, Poseidon, Oceanus, and others. Some have their own names, but since Greek myths have been told and retold over centuries, details get muddled and it can be difficult to tell which nymph is whose daughter. Stories of mermaids and water nymphs often cross over, to the point where they're interchangeable.

Nymph, Tree

a.k.a. Dryad,
Hulder

COMBAT ☼ ☼ ☼ ☼ ☼
MAGIC ☼ ☼ ☼ ☼ ☼
SMARTS ☼ ☼ ☼ ☼ ☼
LOOT ☼ ☼ ☼ ☼ ☼
DANGER ☼ ☼ ☼ ☼ ☼

A female spirit who is the physical manifestation of a tree's soul, dedicated to the protection of the forest. As the nymph is spiritually bound to the tree, if it suffers injury or dies, so does the nymph, and vice versa. Killing a nymph's tree results in a curse being placed on the offender, who will be plagued with bad luck, ruin, and disease. When tree nymphs take on human form, they often have leaves in their hair, an animal's tail, or are completely hollow, having a large hole in their back. Tree nymphs are loved by all the animals in their domain, and normally shy creatures like deer and rabbits may turn vicious to protect them. Magical creatures like unicorns are likely to live in their groves, acting as their most faithful guardians.

Adventurer's Tip: The older the forest, the more powerful the spirits that live within. Stick to forest paths and pick no more flowers than you absolutely need.

Greek mythology has different names for each tree nymph depending on the type of tree it inhabits; dryads live in oak trees, meliai in ash, epimeliads in apple, caryatids in nut trees, daphnaie in laurel, and so on. Japanese tree spirits called kodama are said to inhabit particular trees, and priests mark them out by building shrines at the base or tying thick white ropes around them. The bisan of Malay folklore is a protector of camphor trees, but since she doesn't live in the tree herself, the fairy may allow it to be cut down after she's been given a chicken as a sacrifice.

Ogre

a.k.a. Hill Giant,
Stallo

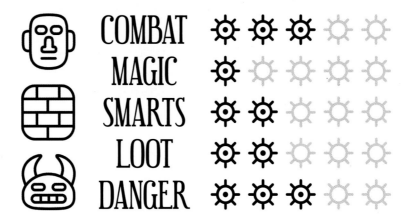

COMBAT ☼ ☼ ☼ ☼ ☼

MAGIC ☼ ☼ ☼ ☼ ☼

SMARTS ☼ ☼ ☼ ☼ ☼

LOOT ☼ ☼ ☼ ☼ ☼

DANGER ☼ ☼ ☼ ☼ ☼

Once a member of a primordial titan race, these brutish creatures are smaller and less intelligent than other giants. Where ancient titans were proud and noble, ogres are but brutish descendants who share little of their ancestors' positive traits. While most giants moved to the edges of the world to continue their civilizations away from humans, ogres opted to stay near to their small usurpers. Ogres live in crude dwellings in forests and hills, occasionally attacking nearby hamlets to steal goods and livestock and eating anybody who would oppose them. Ogre family units are rare and short-lived, as the largest members have a tendency to eat their partners, siblings, and children.

Adventurer's Tip: Though ogres are not craftsmen, their filthy lairs can still contain precious treasure they've plundered from passing caravans.

The term "ogre" comes from Orcus, one of the names of the Roman god of the Underworld. All cultures have a variant on the man-eating giant that lives on the outskirts of society. These cannibalistic bogeymen may have been inspired by fears of carnivorous animals, murderous bandits, general xenophobia, or may even be a demonization of people of above-average height, such as those born with conditions like gigantism or acromelagy. In folklore, ogres and other dim-witted giants were often bested by trickster heroes.

Oni

a.k.a. Akuma,
Mountain Devil

COMBAT	☀ ☀ ☀ ☼ ☼
MAGIC	☀ ☼ ☼ ☼ ☼
SMARTS	☀ ☀ ☼ ☼ ☼
LOOT	☀ ☀ ☀ ☼ ☼
DANGER	☀ ☀ ☀ ☼ ☼

A demonic race appearing as large humanoids with horns, tusks, and brightly colored skin. Though the great majority work in the Underworld as enforcers of divine punishment, rebellious oni have been known to cross into the mortal realm to revel in robbery and murder. Onis tend to travel alone or in pairs, but especially charismatic individuals can assemble masses of monsters into terrifying armies. Oni chieftans can be distinguished by their mode of dress; while common oni tend to wear tiger or bear skins, those in leadership positions bedeck themselves in the finest clothing and armor from their plunder. Oni armies dwell in strongholds atop mountains, cliffs, and islands, which are hidden from human eyes with illusory magic.

Adventurer's Tip: Northeasterly winds are an indication that oni have passed by recently. Prayer can keep them at bay.

Oni are the Japanese equivalent of European giants, demons, and bogeymen, and as such are frequent villains in folktales. Momotaro (Peach Boy) is one of Japan's most famous tales, wherein the eponymous child sets out to defeat an army of oni that have been attacking the countryside. Accompanied by a dog, a monkey, and a pheasant, he sails to Oni Island, where he defeats the devils therein, rescues some damsels, and claims stolen treasure.

186

Ooze

a.k.a. Blob Monster,
Slime

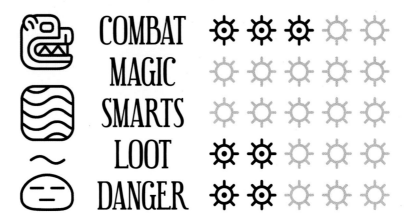

COMBAT	☀	☀	☀	☼	☼
MAGIC	☼	☼	☼	☼	☼
SMARTS	☼	☼	☼	☼	☼
LOOT	☀	☀	☼	☼	☼
DANGER	☀	☀	☼	☼	☼

A gelatinous creature completely focused on eating. The ooze has little to nothing in the way of internal organs, essentially being a crawling mass of stomach acid. It has weak photoreceptors, only being able to visually detect changes in light, so it primarily hunts by sensing vibrations. The surface of an ooze's body is sticky and can be made permeable to absorb and dissolve any suitable organic material. As it eats, it grows, and can achieve massive proportions if its food intake isn't curtailed. This monster's malleable body means that it can easily squeeze into small gaps regardless of how big it gets, including through grates and under doors. Destroying an ooze requires fire, water, or a chemical compound to break up the body, as slicing it will only create two smaller oozes.

Adventurer's Tip: Many adventurers have walked face-first into an ooze, not realizing that what seemed like an empty room was actually filled with a giant monster made of semitransparent acid.

Oozes are likely inspired by amoebae and other microscopic organisms that eat by wrapping themselves around a foreign object (a process called phagocytosis). An early version of this monster appears in 1958's The Blob, *where an alien amoeba terrorizes and consumes a small town. They're common enemies in fantasy games, which include such examples as the gelatinous cube from* Dungeons & Dragons, *the slime from the* Dragon Quest *series, and the flan from the* Final Fantasy *series.*

Ooze, Lava

a.k.a. Fire Blob,
Fire Slime

COMBAT	☀ ☀ ☼ ☼ ☼	
MAGIC	☀ ☀ ☼ ☼ ☼	
SMARTS	☀ ☼ ☼ ☼ ☼	
LOOT	☀ ☀ ☼ ☼ ☼	
DANGER	☀ ☀ ☼ ☼ ☼	

A variant of the ooze, having a body made of magma instead of acidic plasm. While the common ooze primarily feeds on flesh, the lava ooze prefers minerals, melting earth and metal with its extreme heat and fusing it to its own body mass. The belly of this ooze glows white with heat, but its upper surface is cooler, forming a hard crust that occasionally pops with a belch of toxic smoke. Minerals with a higher melting point remain in the ooze's body for a longer period of time, meaning some oozes have clusters of undigestible gems at their core. Its lack of interest in organic matter makes it relatively non-aggressive, but adventurers wearing appetizing armor or jewellery may attract its attention.

Adventurer's Tip: Water evaporates on contact with the lava ooze, but the sudden cooling effect can cause it to become paralyzed or even burst.

Though the land around volcanoes is often lush due to rich soil, no creatures are capable of surviving the high temperatures of magma itself. Deep in the ocean, hydrothermal vents spew out superheated clouds of minerals, reaching temperatures of up to 842°F. These mineral clouds are fed on by bacteria, which are in turn fed on by crustaceans and other invertebrates, making the areas around hydrothermal vents teem with life.

Parasitic Vine

a.k.a. Killer Kudzu

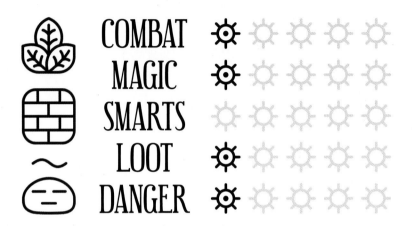

COMBAT ☼ ☼ ☼ ☼ ☼
MAGIC ☼ ☼ ☼ ☼ ☼
SMARTS ☼ ☼ ☼ ☼ ☼
LOOT ☼ ☼ ☼ ☼ ☼
DANGER ☼ ☼ ☼ ☼ ☼

A species of vine that requires an animal host to reproduce. The flowers of the vine produce scents which are attractive to surrounding fauna, allowing the plant to implant them with seeds. Each type of vine has its own way of doing this, whether through fruit, a pollen-filled spray, or seed-bearing thorns that pierce the skin. Regardless of delivery method, the seeds make their way into the body, growing within and eventually taking control of the creature. Hosts are compelled to seek out large population areas whilst neglecting their own need to eat and drink, and turn violent if others try to prevent their mission. Once the creature starves to death, the vine reaches maturity, bursting out of the body and flowering, starting the cycle anew.

Adventurer's Tip: Entire towns have been consumed by this vine. They cannot be rescued. Burn it all to the ground.

While there are many parasitic plants, their hosts are generally other plants. However, there are a number of parasitic fungi that prey on animals, such as Cordyceps, *which infects arthropods. Stricken bugs climb to high places and starve to death, and when the* Cordyceps *blooms, its spores are spread over a wide area. This fungus was the inspiration behind the mushroom-zombies in the 2013 video game* The Last of Us.

Penanggalan

a.k.a. Krasue,
Leyak

COMBAT	☀	☆	☆	☆	☆
MAGIC	☀	☀	☆	☆	☆
SMARTS	☀	☀	☆	☆	☆
LOOT	☀	☀	☆	☆	☆
DANGER	☀	☀	☆	☆	☆

A ghoul that appears as a woman during the day and a severed head with trailing organs at night. Though the penanggalan subsists on blood, it is not an undead vampire, but rather a cursed living woman. She feeds at night, but since her monstrous form is weak, she is forced to seek out corpses, children, and the bed-ridden. She alights on rooftops, and inserts a long sharp tongue through the cracks in the walls and under doors to reach those within. While the head is away, the penanggalan's abandoned body is hollow and defenseless, and the monster must be careful to hide it someplace safe. Her head's trailing organs are also vulnerable, as without the protection of the body, they are likely to get tangled in branches and scratched by thorns.

Adventurer's Tip: If you find the penanggalan's empty body, fill it with broken glass and nails. This will shred the ghoul's organs as it tries to squeeze them back in.

The penanggalan and her variants are monsters appearing in Southeast Asian nations. In human form, they're generally midwives, allowing them access to future victims. Each version has her own dietary requirements, either for flesh, blood, fetuses, or worse. Thailand's version, the krasue, is especially unfortunate since she's cursed with an eternal hunger that drives her to eat feces if no flesh or blood is available.

Peryton

a.k.a. Demon Stag

COMBAT ☼ ☼ ☼ ☼ ☼
MAGIC ☼ ☼ ☼ ☼ ☼
SMARTS ☼ ☼ ☼ ☼ ☼
LOOT ☼ ☼ ☼ ☼ ☼
DANGER ☼ ☼ ☼ ☼ ☼

A mysterious chimeric beast that loathes mankind. Scholarly opinions on the peryton's origins vary wildly; some claim them to be cursed souls, while others claim them to be demons, or else magical beasts or even some kind of magical experiment gone wrong. This confusion likely arises from the peryton's unique ability to cast a human-shaped shadow, which disappears for a brief while after the beast feeds on human blood. The pertyon appears as a confusing amalgamation of stag and bird, always bearing a deer head and wings, but having either two or four limbs in any combination of deer hooves or bird claws. Perytons who have been unable to find prey have been observed eating earth or gnawing on rocks.

Adventurer's Tip: Their inherent hatred of humans make perytons impossible to tame without the use of magical riding gear.

The peryton first appears in Jose Luis Borges' 1950s Book of Imaginary Beings, *supposedly coming from a sixteenth century work, which itself references a lost Greek document. Both ancient texts are fictional. Borges' creation may have been inspired by the hippalectryon, a creature with the front half of a horse and the body and hind legs of a chicken. The peryton also bears some resemblance to the wolpertinger, a German hoax creature often appearing in taxidermy, said to be part deer, bird, squirrel, and rabbit.*

Phoenix

a.k.a. Bennu,
Firebird

COMBAT	☼	☼	☼	☼	○
MAGIC	☼	☼	○	○	○
SMARTS	☼	☼	○	○	○
LOOT	☼	☼	☼	☼	○
DANGER	☼	☼	○	○	○

An immensely rare bird with fiery feathers and a curious life cycle; every few centuries, the phoenix bursts into flames and burns to death. A new phoenix rises from the ashy remains, fully formed and ready to fly. Naturalists debate as to whether this second phoenix is a new individual or the original bird returned to a youthful state. If the second is true, the bird is essentially immortal. Slaying a phoenix doesn't destroy it, but merely triggers the rebirth process. The fiery nature of this bird is reflected in its golden plumage, which glows with solar radiance. The feathers continue to put forth light and heat long after they've been shed, and may start fires if they land on dry material.

Adventurer's Tip: Alchemists pay handsomely for phoenix feathers and ashes, as they're potential ingredients for the Philosopher's Stone and the Elixir of Immortality.

The phoenix was believed by the Ancient Greeks to live in Arabia. Its origins may lie in the Egyptian Bennu, a heronlike creature allied to the sun god Ra. A new Bennu is born from its parent's ashes, which are carried by the younger bird to be entombed in the temple in Heliopolis. The Chinese fenghuang, Japanese ho-oh, and Persian simurgh are associated with the phoenix, but while these are birds of good omen symbolic of the sun and divinity, they do not self-immolate.

Psychopomp

a.k.a. Reaper,
Shinigami

COMBAT ☼ ☼ ☼ ☼ ☼
MAGIC ☼ ☼ ☼ ☼ ☼
SMARTS ☼ ☼ ☼ ☼ ☼
LOOT ☼ ☼ ☼ ☼ ☼
DANGER ☼ ☼ ☼ ☼ ☼

A spirit serving the forces of death, tasked with leading souls into the afterlife. Psychopomps appear when someone is near their time of death, often waiting near deathbeds, in hospitals, or wandering through battlefields. While many people believe the entity does the slaying, it is only there to gather the soul, not kill. Those about to die and the magically gifted can see psychopomps, but no two people seem to agree on what the spirits look like. Their appearance seems to be dictated by how fearful of death the observer is; those who dread it see ominous birds and beasts, skeletal figures, or looming shadows, while those who accept death may see angelic figures, old family members and friends, or some other comforting sight.

Adventurer's Tip: Psychopomps have been known to pursue those astrally projecting or having some other out of body experience, since they naturally assume a soul outside the body is dead.

> *From the Greek* psychopompos, *"guide of souls." The inevitability of death has led to figures who come for the soul being present in all cultures, whether they be the instigators of death, assistants to the soul, or staff in a complex afterlife bureaucracy. Greek myth's Charon literally ferries the souls to Hades, rowing the dead across the river Styx in exchange for a coin and stranding those who were buried without the ferryman's fee. The most famous psychopomp in the West is the Grim Reaper, a scythe-wielding, black-robed skeleton.*

Qilin

a.k.a. Heavenly Unicorn,
Lin

COMBAT	☼	☼	○	○	○
MAGIC	☼	☼	☼	○	○
SMARTS	☼	☼	☼	○	○
LOOT	☼	☼	○	○	○
DANGER	☼	☼	☼	○	○

A scaled horse-like beast, appearing in the mortal world to announce good fortune. The qilin has anywhere between one and three horns and a mane of roiling clouds that turn to flame when worked up into a fury. This is a creature of great gentleness, with a step so light that it walks on grass without bending a blade, on water without making ripples, and on air as if it were flying. The qilin is sometimes summoned to courts to assist judges, as it has the innate ability to tell the truth from lies and the guilty from the innocent. It does not speak and it does no harm to any creature, but it will point to the wicked with its horns and let the court mete out whatever punishment it sees fit.

Adventurer's Tip: Do not injure a qilin, as this angers the gods, who replace auspicious times with drought, famine, and war.

The qilin is a Chinese chimeric beast, with variants in other East Asian countries. Though commonly referred to as the Eastern unicorn, the beast is most often depicted with two horns. The giraffe's strange anatomy and scalelike spots have led it to be associated with the mythical beast, with gilin *and* kirin *meaning "giraffe" in Korean and Japanese, respectively. A similar creature to the qilin was the zhi, a smaller creature who, like the qilin, would be summoned to court, but would actually gore the guilty with its horns.*

Rakshasa

a.k.a. Man-Eater Demon

COMBAT ☼ ☼ ☼ ☼ ☼

MAGIC ☼ ☼ ☼ ☼ ☼

SMARTS ☼ ☼ ☼ ☼ ☼

LOOT ☼ ☼ ☼ ☼ ☼

DANGER ☼ ☼ ☼ ☼ ☼

An animal-headed, demonic race best known for their insurmountable hunger. The first rakshasa were accidentally created from the breath of a sleeping god and were cast down to the mortal world when they tried to eat him. They have since multiplied, hunting humans and decorating their lairs with the skulls of their victims, which the demons use as bowls and cups. Rakshasa are humanoid in shape, but have animal features such as tiger heads, spotted bodies, and horns. Greater rakshasa lords have redundant body parts, with some having up to ten heads. All of these monsters have a basic knowledge of illusory and shapeshifting magic, with their spells being most powerful at night.

Adventurer's Tip: Some rakshasa have been known to turn to the path of good, dedicating themselves to the gods. These repentant demons can provide information to heroes on how to best their evil brethren.

> *Though the term means "demon," the name is derived from Sanskrit* rakshama, *meaning "protect me," the cry uttered by the god Brahma after the newly created beings tried to eat him. In the* Ramayana, *an Indian epic, Rama (the seventh avatar of Vishnu) goes the war with the rakshasa-king Ravana after the demon kidnaps his wife Sita. Among the hero's allies in his battle are the divine monkey-king Hanuman and Vibhishana the enlightened younger brother of the demon lord.*

Redcap

a.k.a. Bloody Cowl

COMBAT ☼ ☼ ☼ ○ ○

MAGIC ☼ ☼ ○ ○ ○

SMARTS ☼ ☼ ☼ ○ ○

LOOT ☼ ☼ ○ ○ ○

DANGER ☼ ☼ ☼ ○ ○

A solitary fairy that wears a cap dyed red with blood. Beneath their hats, redcaps look like evil old men with crooked teeth, scruffy hair, and fiery eyes. Though small, redcaps are deceptively strong, easily overpowering their victims and shrugging off the damage of any weapon levied against them. These wicked fairies like to reside in the abandoned castles and forts of deposed tyrants, being especially attracted the bloody, violent history of these places. They wait for lost travellers to seek shelter in their ruins at night and attack their unsuspecting victims by maiming them with scythes and pikes, kicking them to death with their iron boots, or collapsing the building's loose masonry on them. The fairy then soaks its hat in the blood of his victims, adding their lives to his own.

Adventurer's Tip: Unlike most fairies, redcaps don't fear iron but can still be repelled by prayers and holy symbols. This makes them vanish in a puff of smoke, leaving a single tooth behind.

The redcap is said to live in abandoned castles at the border between England and Scotland. In fairy folklore, the color of the fairy's dress is indicative of its behavior. Gentler, more social fairies (or "trooping" fairies) were said to wear green, while solitary fairies wore red. Though the red-wearing fairies were often more dangerous, this wasn't a universal rule. The original stories of leprechauns actually had them wearing red, and their garb was later changed to green to reflect their association with Ireland, the Emerald Isle.

Roc

a.k.a. Giant Eagle,
Ruhk

COMBAT	☀ ☀ ☀ ☀ ☼	
MAGIC	☼ ☼ ☼ ☼ ☼	
SMARTS	☀ ☼ ☼ ☼ ☼	
LOOT	☀ ☀ ☼ ☼ ☼	
DANGER	☀ ☀ ☀ ☀ ☼	

A giant bird of prey which easily carries large beasts, with their favorite prey being giant snakes, elephants, and whales. The roc hunts by snatching up the chosen victim, flying into the sky, and dropping it onto rocky ground. Their wings are so large that when they're outstretched they can block out the sun, and each flap sounds like a roll of thunder. Rocs live near warm seas, building their nests on cliffs and mountains, often above the cloud line. The nest is constructed from large branches, smaller uprooted trees, and even pieces of wrecked ships, as it must be wide enough to hold both the roc and its titan eggs. Spoiled eggs are pushed out of the nest and have been known to flood cliffside villages with their rotten contents.

Adventurer's Tip: Rocs are very protective of their nests and have been known to attack ships and destroy towns if any of their eggs or fledglings have been harmed.

A creature appearing in Middle Eastern and Indian mythology and fairy tales, and popularized in the West by exaggerating explorers and the translations of The Book of 1001 Nights. *The roc and other folkloric titan birds may have been inspired by now-extinct animals (such as the elephant bird or Haast's eagle) or by fossils of pterosaurs, the flying dinosaurs. Queztalcoaltus* northropi *was the largest of these ancient animals and is theorized to have had a wingspan of up to thirteen meters.*

Salamander

a.k.a. Fire Snake,
Lava Lizard

COMBAT	☀	☀	☀	○	○
MAGIC	☀	○	○	○	○
SMARTS	☀	☀	☀	○	○
LOOT	☀	☀	☀	○	○
DANGER	☀	☀	○	○	○

A lizard or snakelike creature born of fire. Though salamanders can lay eggs, these beasts are related to fire elementals and can spontaneously form from burning material. Salamanders are most likely to appear in volcanoes, deserts, and alchemist's labs. Salamanders that live in houses can be found making their nests in the hearth, feeding on coal, burning wood, and ashes. As they feed, they grow in size, strength, and intelligence, and some have been known to transform into dragons. Their blood is hot and viscous like lava, and dead salamanders can continue to shed heat for days. Leather made from their hide has fire-resistant properties, making it a good material for protective gear.

Adventurer's Tip: With proper care (and a fireproof enclosure), salamanders can be used as living lamps, stoves, and forges.

It's thought that this creature is inspired by real lizards running out of fireplaces. Rather than being formed in the fire, these animals were hiding in the comfortable damp of rotting firewood, fleeing when their homes were added to the flames. Though the modern fantasy salamander is immune to heat because it's made of fire, ancient texts claim the animal was immune because its body was so cold that it would extinguish the flames. Some ancient fireproof garments are said to be woven of salamander wool, but this is actually asbestos fibers.

Satyr

a.k.a. Faun,
Kalkes

COMBAT	✦ ✦ ✧ ✧ ✧
MAGIC	✦ ✧ ✧ ✧ ✧
SMARTS	✦ ✦ ✦ ✧ ✧
LOOT	✦ ✦ ✧ ✧ ✧
DANGER	✦ ✧ ✧ ✧ ✧

A horned nature spirit with the torso of a man and the legs and ears of a goat or horse. Satyrs spend their days running in wild places, drinking, telling crude jokes, playing musical instruments, or otherwise indulging in their hedonistic impulses. Drunken satyrs are extremely lustful and will chase after nymphs, mortals, and animals alike, trying to seduce them with music or wine, until they come across some other entertaining thing or grow bored. Some forest gods have been known to flay overeager satyrs after having receiving complaints from offended nymphs. Though wild satyrs generally cavort in groups across warm fields and forests, they may occasionally erect simple huts as dwellings if they seek more privacy.

Adventurer's Tip: Though hardy drinkers, these fairies are not completely immune to the effects of alcohol. Encourage insistent satyrs to continue drinking, and make your escape when they pass out.

> *A Greek mythological creature and servant to Dionysus, the god of wine. The two most powerful satyrs are Pan, a god in his own right, and Silenus, the tutor of Dionysus. Like many Greek creatures, Pan and the satyrs were adapted into Roman mythology, becoming Faunus and the fauns. Early satyrs were violent lechers, often depicted in artwork as having permanent, monstrous erections. As time passed on, depictions of satyrs softened, with romantic encounters with the creatures being consensual or completely absent.*

Senmurv

a.k.a. Simir,
Simurgh

COMBAT ☼ ☼ ☼ ○ ○

MAGIC ☼ ☼ ☼ ○ ○

SMARTS ☼ ☼ ☼ ○ ○

LOOT ☼ ☼ ☼ ○ ○

DANGER ☼ ☼ ○ ○ ○

A hybrid beast having the body and wings of a great bird and the head and claws of a dog. The senmurv roosts in wondrous trees at the edges of the desert, the branches of which bear every kind of fruit. Though it lives in isolation, the senmurv is a good-hearted beast and has been known to fly over the sands, looking for lost travellers. It shields those it finds from the sun with its wings, brings them food and water, and may even offer to carry them out of the desert on its back. Some senmurv may nurse abandoned human children and, if no parents are to be found, will gladly raise the child as their own. When not helping travellers, the senmurv takes seeds from its tree to scatter about the world.

Adventurer's Tip: The feathers of a senmurv, freely given, can be burned to summon the beast for aid. It knows which plants make the best medicine.

Although this creature of Persian myth is sometimes depicted as having the head of another animal, it's also common to see it as entirely bird-shaped. The senmurv is often considered synonymous with other mythical birds such as the phoenix, griffin, and roc. In the epic of Shahnameh, *a simurgh is tasked by God to raise the infant prince Zál after he's abandoned in the desert for being albino. When spreading the seeds from the tree of life, the senmurv is sometimes aided by the cinamros bird, who gathers up the seeds and gives them to the rain angel Tishtar.*

Serpentfolk

a.k.a. Ophidian

COMBAT ☼ ☼ ☼ ☼ ☼

MAGIC ☼ ☼ ☼ ☼ ☼

SMARTS ☼ ☼ ☼ ☼ ☼

LOOT ☼ ☼ ☼ ☼ ☼

DANGER ☼ ☼ ☼ ☼ ☼

Snakelike humanoids from an ancient civilization, which ruled over an age when reptiles were the dominant species. No two serpentfolk are wholly alike, each one having a mixture of reptilian characteristics; some have a tail, some legs, some no limbs at all, and still others have snakes for hair. Their cities were vast, built around temples bearing bloody altars, from which their sorcerer-kings announced the edicts of dark, primeval gods. Though primitive humans existed at this time, they were but slaves to their reptilian overlords. This great empire was laid waste by some bygone disaster, and now only a few serpentfolk still remain, hiding in the dark corners of the earth, awaiting their chance to wrest back control from humankind.

Adventurer's Tip: Though sometimes confused with naga, serpentfolk are far from divine. While they can be powerful foes, they are nevertheless mortal.

There are many myths of supernatural snake-human hybrids, but most of them are regarded as mystical demigods or devils. The concept of snake-people as a race akin to humans is more recent, appearing in early pulp fiction such as Robert E. Howard's Conan the Barbarian *series of short stories, and remains popular in science fiction and fantasy. A modern conspiracy theory insists that the world is ruled by alien reptilians who have disguised themselves as world leaders to enslave or destroy mankind.*

Shedu

a.k.a. Lamassu,
Winged Bull

COMBAT	☼	☼	☼	☼	☼
MAGIC	☼	☼	☼	☼	☼
SMARTS	☼	☼	☼	☼	☼
LOOT	☼	☼	☼	☼	☼
DANGER	☼	☼	☼	☼	☼

A heavenly beast appearing as a winged bull with a human face. Shedim are often confused with sphinxes, but the resemblance is only superficial, as these creatures are faithful servants to the gods, making them more akin to angels. They carry the thrones of deities, draw their chariots, and are sometimes sent to the mortal world to assist or punish humans. Though they generally reside among the stars, many live permanently in the physical world to be the eternal guardians of cities and tombs. Whilst among humans, shedim may turn invisible in order to act as unseen watchers over their charges. Earthbound shedim can be consulted as oracles, since they can divine the will of the gods by reading the stars and planets.

Adventurer's Tip: The shedu guards its assigned city long after it has fallen into ruin, and continues to stand by the doorways to stop intruders.

A creature of Assyrian mythology, also sometimes called a lamassu. There is little mention of them in ancient texts, existing primarily as stone reliefs in ruins, leaving scholars to debate over their abilities and even their gender (sometimes a shedu is male and a lamassu female; other times they're both male). The Bull of Heaven sent to earth by the goddess Ishtar to get revenge on Gilgamesh may have been a shedu.

Soul Cage

a.k.a. Cage Demon

COMBAT	☼	☼	☼	○	○
MAGIC	☼	☼	☼	○	○
SMARTS	☼	☼	○	○	○
LOOT	☼	☼	☼	☼	○
DANGER	☼	☼	☼	☼	○

A creature with a hollow, cagelike torso, in which it can trap both the physical living and the intangible dead. Victims imprisoned in this way are then conveyed to the soul cage's master, or else remain on display as a warning to others. The prisoner trapped within slowly withers and fades as this monster consumes its soul. Soul cages are frequently employed by demons and witches to track down those who would look to break unholy contracts. Many also work for death gods as psychopomps, ferrying the dead from one part of the Underworld to another. Even then, both witches and gods must be careful not to allow the cage to carry too many souls at any given time, since the more souls a cage has, the more powerful it becomes.

Adventurer's Tip: The torso of this demon is equipped with a door that can only be opened from the outside, but many soul cages keep it padlocked.

> *While there are several legends of humans being trapped in the bellies of monsters and demons, the visual of the cage-bodied creature is more modern. Beings of this sort often make grisly visual reference to a ribcage—a "cage" of bone keeping the heart, lungs, and other essential organs safe within. Though often depicted as monstrous, more humorous or surreal depictions exist, such as the birdcage bird from Disney's* Alice in Wonderland.

Sphinx

a.k.a. Androsphinx,
Gynosphinx

COMBAT	☀	☀	☀	○	○
MAGIC	☀	○	○	○	○
SMARTS	☀	☀	☀	☀	○
LOOT	☀	☀	○	○	○
DANGER	☀	☀	☀	○	○

A beast of great intellect, having a lion's body, eagle wings, and a human face, often female. When not resting in their well-hidden lairs, sphinxes lurk by isolated roads or on the outskirts of cities. They stop any travellers passing by, threatening them with death unless they engage in the sphinxes' challenges, whether physical contests or thought exercises. Those who fail to best the sphinx are then gleefully devoured by the smug monster. Sphinxes are especially proud of their riddles, spending weeks choosing the right words for a puzzle. Their confidence is crushed when a riddle is solved, causing the sphinx to bluster and slink away in embarrassment, though some poor sports have been known to eat their opponents anyway.

Adventurer's Tip: Some sphinxes have been observed skulking in libraries, seeking to broaden their knowledge and improve their riddles.

Though the earliest known sphinxes appear in Ancient Egyptian art, the riddling sphinx was made famous in Oedipus Rex, *a Greek play by Sophocles, wherein the monster kills herself when the protagonist Oedipus correctly answers her problem. The purushamriga of India is a similar sphinxlike monster, who challenges the hero Bhima to a race, threatening to eat the human if able to catch him. Though not as cerebral a challenge as its Greek counterpart, the purushamriga is nevertheless bested by Bhima, though this beast accepts its defeat with good grace.*

Sphinx, Crio

a.k.a. Heavenly Ram,
Ram-Headed Sphinx

COMBAT	☼ ☼ ☼ ☼ ☼
MAGIC	☼ ☼ ☼ ☼ ☼
SMARTS	☼ ☼ ☼ ☼ ☼
LOOT	☼ ☼ ☼ ☼ ☼
DANGER	☼ ☼ ☼ ☼ ☼

A lesser sphinx-type beast, having the body of a lion, the head of a ram, and sometimes wings. The criosphinx's animal head hints at the fact that it is of lower intelligence than its humanheaded relative and, as such, will not pause for games, riddles, or debates with travellers. In fact, these beasts used to serve a purpose similar to the shedim, being the servants of ancient ramheaded gods. It is possible that they were more intelligent in the past, when they actively had tasks to perform. These old gods have since disappeared, leaving the criosphinxes without purpose; they now either wander the wilds or spend their time in abandoned temples, awaiting their masters' return.

Adventurer's Tip: Though the criosphinxes are not terribly active beasts, they will attack if they feel their territories are encroached upon.

> *From the Greek words* kreos *("ram") and* sphingos *("strangler"). These monsters are actually Egyptian and only have a Greek name due to Herodotus, an ancient Greek historian who described the statues of the beasts in his writings. Reclining criosphinxes and hieracosphinxes (which were hawk-headed) line an avenue of the Egyptian temple of Amun in Karnak. The creator god Amun, along with fertility deities Khnum and Heryshaf, were often depicted with ram heads.*

Spiderfolk

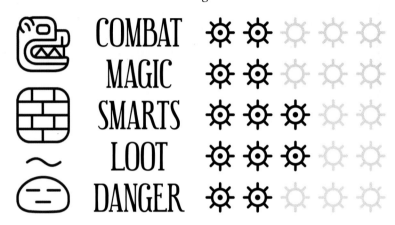

a.k.a. Spider Spirit,
Tsuchigumo

COMBAT	☀ ☀ ☼ ☼ ☼
MAGIC	☀ ☀ ☼ ☼ ☼
SMARTS	☀ ☀ ☀ ☼ ☼
LOOT	☀ ☀ ☀ ☼ ☼
DANGER	☀ ☀ ☼ ☼ ☼

A rarely-seen race of giant spiders with human faces, master weavers of both web and illusion. They are descendants of the ancient arachnids that were present during the construction of the universe and benefit from secret knowledge that has been passed down from spider to spider for thousands of years. Because of this, spiderfolk can integrate the very threads of reality into their web-spinning, allowing them to create illusions, hypnotic patterns, and even bridges between dimensions. Spiderfolk who carelessly forget to dismantle their bridges when they finish using them may end up creating pathways that can be used both by mortals and creatures from strange places beyond this world.

Adventurer's Tip: The shimmering silk from these spiders' webs can be used to make invisibility cloaks and other magical garments.

The spider is an important figure in North American, African, and Oceanian legends, appearing as a good creator god (such as Grandmother Spider and Areop-Enap) or a neutral trickster spirit (like Iktomi and Anansi). Arachnophobia, the fear of spiders, has led to these animals generally being represented as evil—or at least unpleasant—in most media. Still, kindly fictional spiders appear on occasion, such as Charlotte from Charlotte's Web, *who saves Wilbur the pig from slaughter by weaving words into her webs.*

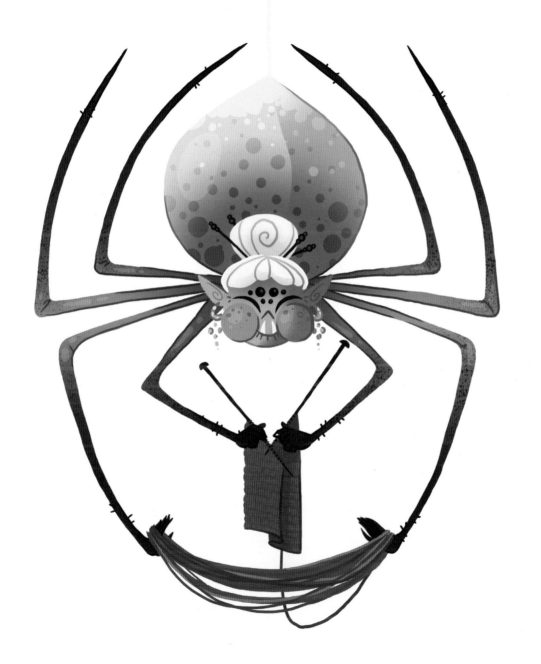

Spriggan

a.k.a. Fairy Brute

COMBAT ☼ ☼ ☼ ☼ ☼

MAGIC ☼ ☼ ☼ ☼ ☼

SMARTS ☼ ☼ ☼ ☼ ☼

LOOT ☼ ☼ ☼ ☼ ☼

DANGER ☼ ☼ ☼ ☼ ☼

A scowling fairy, tasked by fairy lords to guard treasure, often living in large groups in hollow trees, ruins, or graves. Their main power is having the ability to alter their size, one moment being small enough to slip between the cracks in masonry, the next moment swelling up to the size of giants. Often the sight of dozens of tiny men streaming out from a barrow-mound is enough to scare away any would-be graverobbers. Even under threat of reprisal by fairy monarchs, spriggans can't help growing bored with their assigned tasks and often slip away to cause mischief in nearby farms or towns. They steal items, rocks, and cattle from humans, and bring them back to their hiding places to add to the hoard.

Adventurer's Tip: Don't even remove so much as a stone from a tomb guarded by spriggans, as bad luck will follow you until it is returned.

The spriggan is a fairy creature of Cornish legend, its name coming from spyrys *("spirit"). They share many attributes with the other "little people" that make up the fairy tribes of England, Scotland, Wales, and Ireland, but are most notable for their bad temper. Because of this fairy's ability to grow so large, it was also thought that spriggans were the ghosts of giants, another monster of Cornish legend.*

Succubus

a.k.a. Incubus,
Sex Demon

COMBAT ✸ ✸ ✶ ✶ ✶
MAGIC ✸ ✸ ✸ ✶ ✶
SMARTS ✸ ✸ ✸ ✶ ✶
LOOT ✸ ✸ ✸ ✶ ✶
DANGER ✸ ✸ ✸ ✶ ✶

A demon that assaults humans in their sleep, leading to mysterious pregnancies. Most demons are created from the manipulation of evil energy or the twisting of damned souls, and only a few are able to produce offspring biologically. The succubus is a type of demonic creature which has developed a way to imitate the reproductive process. The name "succubus" actually only applies when the demon takes on female form to steal seed from a male victim, either by attacking them in their sleep or seducing them. It then transforms into a male form (an incubus) to transfer that seed into a female target. Children born from this unholy intervention are called cambions: magically gifted, prone to evil, and often bearing some deformity such as tails, hooves, or horns.

Adventurer's Tip: Constant nightmares and lethargy are signs of recurring visits from these demons. Men tend to die from exhaustion, and women may not survive the demon-child's birth.

Sources disagree on whether the succubus and incubus are two different creatures or a single shapeshifting demon. Though the succubus/incubus itself originates in Abrahamic lore, other myths and religions have their own demons similarly associated with sexual voraciousness and night attacks. During sleep paralysis, a state by which a person is awake, but the body is frozen as if asleep, the person may hallucinate monstrous figures attacking them.

231

Tarasque

a.k.a. Kaijū

COMBAT ☼ ☼ ☼ ☼ ☼
MAGIC ☼ ☼ ☼ ☼ ☼
SMARTS ☼ ☼ ☼ ☼ ☼
LOOT ☼ ☼ ☼ ☼ ☼
DANGER ☼ ☼ ☼ ☼ ☼

A colossal creature, either an animal from primordial times or a new beast brought about by misused alchemy and magic. The tarasque spends centuries in a dormant state, slumbering deep beneath the earth or waters. This calm is punctuated by the landscape-altering devastation brought about when the monster is roused by hunger. Mountains are born when it bursts from the ground, and new rivers and lakes are carved out as it drags itself across the earth. A tarasque can't be killed; it has an impenetrable shell, with both weapons and magic bouncing harmlessly off it, and any damage that is somehow dealt to it quickly heals. Whole cities and forests are devoured before the tarasque's hunger is satisfied and it returns to its long sleep.

Adventurer's Tip: Some cults seem to want to awaken the tarasque, hoping that the ensuing destruction will lead to a new world order.

The legendary tarasque was a dragon that terrorized a town in southern France, immune to all weaponry, but eventually tamed by the prayers of Saint Martha. When she brought the gentle beast to the townsfolk, they panicked and killed it. The town renamed itself Tarascon, which exists to this day. Giant monsters had a resurgence in popularity in twentieth century cinema, with the kaijū genre of Japanese film being entirely dedicated to giant monsters either destroying cities or fighting other giant monsters. Godzilla, a giant radioactive reptile, is the most famous of these kaijū.

233

Tengu

a.k.a. Crow Spirit

COMBAT	☼ ☼ ☼ ☼ ☼
MAGIC	☼ ☼ ☼ ☼ ☼
SMARTS	☼ ☼ ☼ ☼ ☼
LOOT	☼ ☼ ☼ ☼ ☼
DANGER	☼ ☼ ☼ ☼ ☼

A spirit race appearing as clawed, winged humanoids, with either the head of a crow or that of a red-skinned man with an absurdly long nose. The oldest tengu were once human priests and master swordsmen but were transformed into this shape for being overly proud. For this reason, tengu primarily live in the mountains and forests surrounding isolated monasteries, as they bear a grudge towards holy men and warrior-monks. These monsters harass the priests by disturbing their prayers, stealing their things, and tricking them into eating filth. Many a monastery has found itself abandoned as its residents flee their winged harassers. Without monks to torment, tengu turn their troublesome attention to passing travellers.

Adventurer's Tip: Tengu are proficient fighters and will teach their martial arts to those who seek them out in exchange for fish or small cakes.

A popular creature in Japanese folklore, having roots in Chinese myth. The original creature was the tian-gou, a black dog with a fiery tail, and was adopted by Japan as such. At some point it transformed from a dog to a crow-man (the karasu *tengu). Its beak was sometimes replaced with a long nose, eventually leading to the interpretation of the tengu as having an old man's face (the* hanataka *tengu). Though the tengu of older stories are damned souls of priests, modern interpretations often present them as mischievous mountain protectors.*

Timekeeper

a.k.a. Chrono-Custodian,
Time Guardian

COMBAT	☼ ☼ ☼ ☼ ☼
MAGIC	☼ ☼ ☼ ☼ ☼
SMARTS	☼ ☼ ☼ ☼ ☼
LOOT	☼ ☼ ☼ ☼ ☼
DANGER	☼ ☼ ☼ ☼ ☼

A physical manifestation of the space-time continuum tasked with maintaining its stability. Though timekeepers are all-knowing four-dimensional beings, they possess no empathy or emotion, seeing living things simply as objects to be kept in their proper temporal place. These guardians travel back and forth through time unseen, untangling minor paradoxes and keeping track of archmages and other magically potent beings that could pose a threat to the fabric of reality. Timekeepers are beyond divinity and would attack the gods if they felt it was necessary for the good of the universe. They are constantly battling the erosion of the timeline caused by extradimensional parasites, beings that chew through patches of reality, potentially erasing important events.

Adventurer's Tip: Feelings of déja vu are actually recollections of alternate timelines that timekeepers have since erased.

The concept of beings who watch over destiny is ancient, with the theme of the futility of escaping one's fate being common in Greek legends. With the modern concepts of alternate dimensions and time travel, science fiction shows such as Doctor Who *often give this guardianship of time to organizations of alien beings with near-magical technology. The philosophy of fatalism, a form of determinism, argues that all future actions are determined by past events and that free will and control over our lives is therefore impossible.*

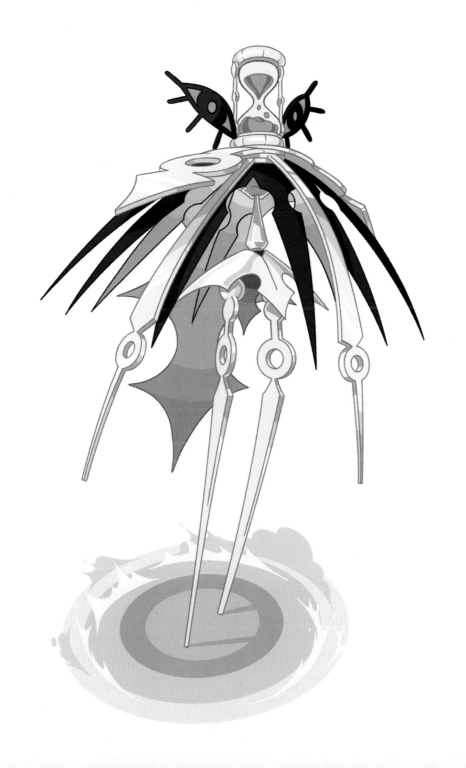

Titan Moth

a.k.a. Moonlit Butterfly

COMBAT ☼ ☼ ☼ ☼ ☼

MAGIC ☼ ☼ ☼ ☼ ☼

SMARTS ☼ ☼ ☼ ☼ ☼

LOOT ☼ ☼ ☼ ☼ ☼

DANGER ☼ ☼ ☼ ☼ ☼

A very rare, very beautiful insect native to the fairy lands. Titan moths are as large as elephants, and the colors of their wings are bright and vibrant, even in the dark, constantly exuding a shimmering light. This shimmer is actually from tiny scales being shed from their wings, an especially potent form of fairy dust that can cause hallucinations, feelings of euphoria, and even death-like sleep. The caterpillar stage of this animal is considerably more dangerous than its adult form, since it is extremely voracious. This is of little consequence in the fairy world, since the plants of those lands are both infinitely bountiful and nourishing. However, if a caterpillar makes its way to the mortal plane, they will devour whole forests in mere days.

Adventurer's Tip: Titan moths can be trained as mounts, but their delicate wings are fragile and easily torn by more vicious flying beasts like dragons and griffins.

While most of today's bugs are very small, fossil records show that insects of exceptional size existed in the Carboniferous and Permian periods (365 to 295 million years ago), with the ancient Meganeura dragonfly having a wingspan over twenty-seven inches across. For comparison, the widest wingspan of any currently living insect belongs to the ghost moth at twelve inches. It's theorized that the prehistoric world's high oxygen levels allowed arthropods to grow larger than they can today.

Treant

a.k.a. Treebeard,
Treefolk

COMBAT	☼	☼	☼	☼	☼
MAGIC	☼	☼	☼	☼	☼
SMARTS	☼	☼	☼	☼	☼
LOOT	☼	☼	☼	☼	☼
DANGER	☼	☼	☼	☼	☼

A tree that has matured into sentience and guards the forest. These plants first develop facelike growths on their bark allowing them to speak, then are able to move their branches as arms, and finally can uproot themselves to walk. Though these living trees are sluggish and loath to move, they are fiercely defensive of their forests and whole groves of treants will gladly rise up to protect them. As treants grow even older, they reenter a dormant state, hardly ever moving but still capable of speech. These ancients become inconceivably wise, accumulating knowledge through centuries of meditation. However, they are so slow-speaking that listeners often lose interest and wander off before the treant gets to the point.

Adventurer's Tip: Treants can influence nearby common plants and trees, encouraging them to grow over paths or strike out at interlopers.

Intelligent and oracular trees appear in a number of the world's mythologies and folklores. As trees are slow-growing, any especially large tree would be assumed to either have become wise and magical over time or been blessed by a god (as in the case of Zeus and the trees of Dodona). Walking trees were popularized by the Ents of J.R.R. Tolkien's The Lord of the Rings, *who assist the heroes, and they remain a popular trope in fantasy media.*

Troll

a.k.a. Earth Giant,
Night-Troll

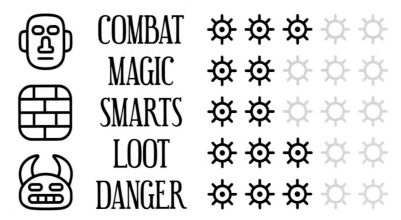

COMBAT	☼ ☼ ☼ ☼ ☼
MAGIC	☼ ☼ ☼ ☼ ☼
SMARTS	☼ ☼ ☼ ☼ ☼
LOOT	☼ ☼ ☼ ☼ ☼
DANGER	☼ ☼ ☼ ☼ ☼

A relative of the earth elementals, often mistaken for a giant. The troll's body is rocklike, with swords and arrows easily glancing off their craggy, hard hides. Bright sunlight has a petrifying effect on these monsters, causing their bodies to completely turn to stone, rendering them lifeless statues. To avoid this, trolls mainly live in deep caves and ravines, only coming out to the surface world at night. Younger or less cautious trolls may go out on overcast or rainy days, but may find their muscles growing stiff from even the dimmed sunlight. Trolls intensely dislike holy places and human habitations and try to destroy these locations by hurling rocks at them. Trolls come in a variety of sizes, from as small as a pebble to as large as a house.

Adventurer's Tip: There are some varieties of trolls that are able to survive sunlight, though their eyes are still blinded by its brightness.

Trolls are creatures of Norse and Scandinavian legend, folkloric descendants of the ancient jötunn. A number of rock formations in these northern countries are said to either have been built by trolls or even be the monsters transformed by the rising sun. Their depiction in legends varies, being either cannibalistic giants or smaller fairies prone to kidnapping children and leaving changelings. Modern versions of the trolls may be friendly and immune to the sunlight curse, such as those in Tove Jansson's Moomins *books and the* Troll Dolls *toy line.*

Unicorn

a.k.a. Catazonon,
Shadhavar

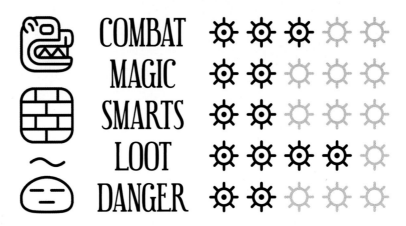

COMBAT	☼	☼	☼	☼	☼
MAGIC	☼	☼	☼	☼	☼
SMARTS	☼	☼	☼	☼	☼
LOOT	☼	☼	☼	☼	☼
DANGER	☼	☼	☼	☼	☼

A horselike creature of delicate and noble bearing, with a single horn protruding from its head. Though the unicorn can seem dainty, this animal is extremely fierce and aggressive, attacking beasts and men. Unicorns seem to have a special hatred for lions, attacking them on sight and becoming locked in gory combat. This animal's fierce nature can be soothed by virgin women, in whose presence they may consent to the riding harness. Unicorns now mostly exist in fairy lands, as mortals have hunted these animals to near-extinction. The beast's horn—also called an alicorn—has the power to negate all poisons, so cups made from this material are in high demand by any person who may fear assassination.

Adventurer's Tip: A line drawn in the earth with a unicorn's horn cannot be crossed by venomous creatures or other poison-bearers.

> *A European creature whose name literally means "one horn," said to live in distant lands. It appears in heraldry, symbolizing purity and valor. Their horns were sold for medicinal purposes, somewhat fraudulently since they were often actually narwhal tusks. Unicorns may have been inspired by sightings of gazelle, deer, and goats with missing horns, or by explorers describing the rhinoceros. The okapi, a relative of the giraffe, was discovered by European explorers searching African forests for unicorns.*

Vampire

a.k.a. Nosferatu,
Strigoi

COMBAT	☼ ☼ ☼ ○ ○
MAGIC	☼ ☼ ☼ ○ ○
SMARTS	☼ ☼ ☼ ○ ○
LOOT	☼ ☼ ○ ○ ○
DANGER	☼ ☼ ☼ ☼ ○

A person who was especially evil in life, rising after death to feed on the living. The vampire leaves its grave at night to attack mortals, biting their necks to drink their blood, growing horribly red and engorged after feeding. Victims are infected by the vampire's bite, becoming their suggestible slaves and transforming into undead spawn when they die. Among their unholy powers are the ability to fly, hypnotize, and transform into animals or mist. These monsters must be careful to return to their graves before dawn, as the divine light of the sun causes them to burst into flames. Even when reduced to ashes, the vampire isn't truly dead, as it can be revived by pouring fresh blood on its dusty remains.

Adventurer's Tip: Staking a vampire doesn't actually kill it, but merely pins it down and makes it unable to move or transform.

Most cultures have their own version of vampires, whether it was a demon, witch, or an undead person. If a grave was suspected of harboring a vampire, it would be dug up and the corpse within mutilated in various ways to prevent it from rising, such as breaking its legs, pinning it down with stakes, or cutting off its head. The vampire in modern fiction is much more suave than its beastly ancestor, imbued with cunning and sexual allure in nighteenth and twentieth century novels like Polidori's The Vampyre, *Le Fanu's* Carmilla, *and Stoker's* Dracula.

Wendigo

a.k.a. Chenoo,
Ice Ghoul

COMBAT	☼ ☼ ☼ ⚙ ⚙	
MAGIC	☼ ☼ ⚙ ⚙ ⚙	
SMARTS	☼ ☼ ⚙ ⚙ ⚙	
LOOT	☼ ☼ ⚙ ⚙ ⚙	
DANGER	☼ ☼ ☼ ⚙ ⚙	

A type of ghoul that appears as a bone-thin giant, covered in blood-matted fur and missing its lips, as if it has gnawed them off in hunger. When snow and ice make it impossible to hunt and stored food runs out, desperate people may turn to cannibalism in order to survive, an abhorrent act that drives the cannibal mad and transforms them into a wendigo. The monster shambles through the wilderness, searching for humans to eat; then when it spots its prey, it launches itself at the victim, charging at them with such speed that its feet don't seem to touch the ground. The wendigo can only be destroyed by chopping up its body into pieces, extracting its heart of solid ice, and melting all these parts in a fire.

Adventurer's Tip: A wendigo may choose to become human again by drinking boiling tallow, an extremely painful process that causes it to vomit up evil vermin.

The wendigo appears in the folklore of the indigenous people of northeastern parts of America. There is a psychological condition called Wendigo psychosis, by which people starving during the winter are overcome by murderous impulses compelling them to kill and eat their companions. This is a controversial condition, with some professionals calling it a fabrication. Regardless, people have eaten their dead or killed others for food in times of famine, an action that inevitably leaves psychological scars.

249

Werecrocodile

a.k.a. Crocothrope,
Manigator

COMBAT	☀	☀	☀	☼	☼	
MAGIC	☀	☼	☼	☼	☼	
SMARTS	☀	☀	☀	☼	☼	
LOOT	☀	☀	☼	☼	☼	
DANGER	☀	☀	☀	☼	☼	

A person who by magical means is able to turn themselves into a crocodile or human-crocodile hybrid. A werecrocodile is generally a witch or other spellcaster who lives in swamps or by rivers. In its reptilian form, it appears as a crocodile of unusual size with an especially cunning glint in its eye, and all other crocodiles and lizards fear and obey it. These werebeasts have been known to accept assassination jobs from human clients who wish to do away with a spouse or enemy, but they delight in murder either way, happily spending their time hunting for bathers and fishermen to devour. Its semi-aquatic nature makes it difficult to catch when in the water, as it will simply dive under the murk to vanish from sight.

Adventurer's Tip: Though slower on land when in animal form, werecrocodiles can still put on sudden bursts of speed to close the distance between them and their target.

Werecrocodiles appear in the folklore of the East Indies and parts of Africa, where the crocodile is an apex predator. In superstitious areas of Zambia, the belief in witches who can control crocodiles or take on their form persists, with sometimes tragic consequences for those accused of performing this dark magic. A legend in the United States tells of Uncle Monday, a witch doctor who escaped slavery and lived with the Seminole tribe. To evade capture, he transformed himself into an alligator and is said to still live in the swamps.

Wereshark

a.k.a. Man-Shark

COMBAT	☼	☼	☼	○	○
MAGIC	☼	☼	○	○	○
SMARTS	☼	☼	☼	○	○
LOOT	☼	☼	○	○	○
DANGER	☼	☼	☼	○	○

A person who by magical means is able to turn themselves into a shark or human-shark hybrid. Whether it is possible to become a wereshark due to a bite is unknown; any victim who survives the initial attack either drowns trying to escape or is too mauled to live. Weresharks are born from unions between humans and sea spirits, with the child doomed to a life of struggling between human expectations and wild impulses. Even when in human form, the person retains the serrated teeth and excellent swimming skills of their piscine aspect. Weresharks always know where good fishing is and ordinary sharks flee from them. These qualities would make them a boon to any coastal village, were it not for the wereshark's insatiable craving for flesh.

Adventurer's Tip: Though sharks can be dangerous, few actually attack humans for food. A sudden uptick in shark attacks is likely the work of a wereshark rather than its mundane cousin.

A Hawaiian legend tells of Nanaue, the child of the human Kalei and the shark king Kamohoalii. Born with a shark's mouth on his back, the shark king warned Kalei never to let her son eat meat. Of course, this prohibition was broken—leading to Nanaue's descent into cannibalism. Stories vary as to whether it was Nanaue's mother or his human grandfather who allowed him to eat meat. Though Japanese legend tells of the samebito ("shark-man"), these are sharklike mermaids rather than weresharks.

Werewolf

*a.k.a. Loup-Garou,
Lycanthrope*

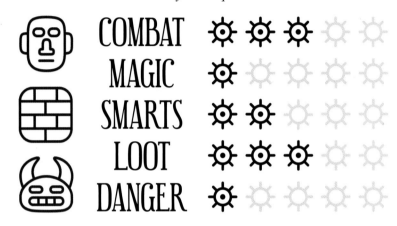

COMBAT ☼ ☼ ☼ ☼ ☼

MAGIC ☼ ☼ ☼ ☼ ☼

SMARTS ☼ ☼ ☼ ☼ ☼

LOOT ☼ ☼ ☼ ☼ ☼

DANGER ☼ ☼ ☼ ☼ ☼

A person who by magical means is able to turn themselves into a wolf or human-wolf hybrid. One can choose to become a werewolf through evil spells, but people who are especially violent and sinful may be stricken by the curse of lycanthropy. At night, the person transforms into a large wolf and prowls around looking for victims, be they animal or human. They rarely eat their prey, only savaging them before moving on, leaving them to bleed to death. Those unlucky enough to survive the attack are cursed to become werewolves themselves. The person may be cured of their curse with silver, wolfsbane, holy symbols, or exorcism, casting out the evil inside them. These methods will likely also kill the person, but their soul will be saved.

Adventurer's Tip: Be sure to burn a werewolf's corpse after it's killed, as werewolves are among those people likely to rise as vampires.

A monster common in European folklore and other places where wolves are apex predators. Though few legends say that werewolves transformed under the full moon and could be killed by silver, modern media has cemented this as a rule. Among the first legendary werewolves was King Lycaon of Greek myth, who tried to feed human flesh to the god Zeus and was transformed into a wolf-man for his crimes. In the Poetic Edda, *the heroes Sigmund and Sinfjotli were transformed into man-eating wolves after donning cursed wolf pelts.*

Will o' the Wisp

a.k.a. Fairy Fire,
Hinkypunk

COMBAT ☼ ☼ ☼ ☼ ☼
MAGIC ☼ ☼ ☼ ☼ ☼
SMARTS ☼ ☼ ☼ ☼ ☼
LOOT ☼ ☼ ☼ ☼ ☼
DANGER ☼ ☼ ☼ ☼ ☼

A strange swinging fire appearing in misty swamps, fields, and forests, that looks like a lamp in the distance signalling to lost travellers. Any people fooled by the will o' the wisp will be led through countless brambles and stagnant waters as the wisp disappears here and reappears there. By the time the morning comes, they find themselves even further from their destination than before, with only the tittering laughter of the unseen wisps for company. Those travellers should count themselves lucky, as especially sadistic wisps have been known to guide people into quicksand and even off cliffs. The supernatural nature of the will o' the wisp can be gleaned from its unnatural colors, as fairy fires burn blue, green, or some other hue not present in common flames.

Adventurer's Tip: People who are liked by the fairies can trust the will o' the wisp, as they'll lead the lucky person to shelter or show them where treasure is buried.

Strange floating lights are sometimes seen in humid environments and have often been given supernatural origins by way of explanation. Often they're depicted as wandering souls or the light created by some monster or witch, though some Eastern and Northern European superstitions have them as marking the location of buried treasure. This phenomenon has a number of scientific explanations, including ball lightning, incandescent gases caused by decaying material, or bioluminescent arthropods and fungi.

Worm-That-Walks

a.k.a. Swarm-Witch,
Verminous King

COMBAT	☀ ☀ ☼ ☼ ☼
MAGIC	☀ ☀ ☀ ☀ ☼
SMARTS	☀ ☀ ☀ ☀ ☼
LOOT	☀ ☀ ☀ ☀ ☼
DANGER	☀ ☀ ☀ ☀ ☀

A creature that appears whole, but is in fact made up of thousands, if not millions, of squirming worms and bugs. Many monstrous beings are able to transform into swarms of animals, but with the worm-that-walks, the swarm is its true form. Mortals may become this monster through especially evil spells, attaining a gruesome form of immortality by encouraging hordes of vermin to eat their body and transferring their soul into the gorged animals. The spellcaster lives on within the swarm, which knits itself into human shape and is further disguised with heavy robes, illusions, or even a false skin. Cutting into the sorcerer betrays the disguise, as wounds produce no blood, instead oozing maggots and jelly.

Adventurer's Tip: If even a single worm survives the destruction of the swarm, the soul of the worm-that-walks survives and can reform its body anew. Use fire to kill them all.

In nature, animals made up of multiple different organisms are called colonial organisms. Such creatures include the Portuguese man o' war, which looks like a jellyfish but is actually made up of several different species of zooids existing symbiotically. Though not a colonial organism, ants may sometimes come together into an interlocking mass to create bridges and islands to survive flooding. Though this process may kill some of the ants, the rest of the colony is saved. The trope of the monster made out of rats or bugs appears in fantasy, science fiction, and horror.

Wyvern

a.k.a. Guivre,
Jaculus

COMBAT	✹	✹	✹	☼	☼
MAGIC	✹	✹	☼	☼	☼
SMARTS	✹	☼	☼	☼	☼
LOOT	✹	✹	☼	☼	☼
DANGER	✹	✹	✹	☼	☼

The gangly, dim-witted cousins of true dragons, wyverns are somewhat batlike in appearance, having only two hind legs and a pair of wings. Though lacking the ability to breathe fire or poison, the tail of a wyvern comes equipped with a venomous barb and their blood is still highly toxic. Though smaller and less intelligent than dragons, wyverns display a capability for spite and cruelty that is suggestive of a sentience beyond that of a mere animal. Warlords are keen to train these monsters as warbeasts and mounts for their armies, as ownership of a "dragon" (or at least a creature that passes for one) is a sure sign of any despot's power. Since wild adult wyverns are too vicious and willful to properly train, it's best to steal eggs from nests and hatch the animal oneself.

Adventurer's Tip: Wyverns are soothed by music, so riders are encouraged to carry horns to calm the beast should it start to misbehave.

> *A European monster whose name is likely a corruption of the Latin* vipera *("viper"). In early art in the West, any kind of vaguely reptilian monster could be classified as a dragon, regardless of other physical traits. Heraldry is possibly the first place where wyverns were set apart, officially being defined as having two legs and two wings. Other subdivisons of dragonkind into linnorm, drake, wyrm, and so on are modern attempts at classifying a highly varied and ancient monster.*

Zaratan

a.k.a. Aspidochelon,
Turtle Island

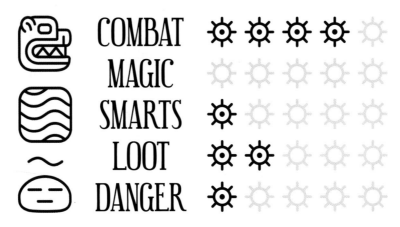

COMBAT ☼ ☼ ☼ ☼ ☼
MAGIC ☼ ☼ ☼ ☼ ☼
SMARTS ☼ ☼ ☼ ☼ ☼
LOOT ☼ ☼ ☼ ☼ ☼
DANGER ☼ ☼ ☼ ☼ ☼

A giant sea turtle whose shell above the waterline is large enough to act as an island. The zaratan spends most of its life dozing at the water's surface, its head submerged to lazily feed on passing fish. Over time, dirt accumulates on the shell, then plants, and later still animals. Even humans have been known to make villages on these moving islands, assuming it to be a magical landmass rather than a living creature. The layer of earth and the turtle's thick shell mean that it doesn't feel the small creatures living on its back. However, the zaratan may be roused from its slumber when ignorant settlers try to mine into its shell in search of metal or fresh water, and the animal rids itself of its pesky stowaways by diving completely beneath the water.

Adventurer's Tip: If you find out you're living on a zaratan, cultivate a good relationship with the animal and it will always lead you to calm waters and good fishing.

> *There are numerous legends of turtles creating the world or transforming themselves into islands to rescue drowning people. In a Lenape creation myth, the world was all water until dry land was created by the Great Spirit, who commanded the Turtle to the surface of the water to have his back covered with mud carried up from the ocean depths by the Muskrat. The concept of living islands may have been brought about by sights of basking whales or landmasses that disappeared and reappeared with the tides.*

Zombie

a.k.a. Living Dead

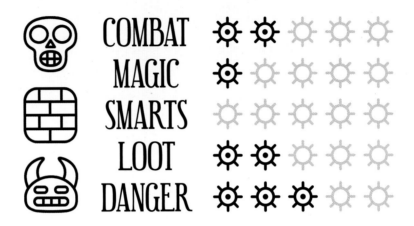

COMBAT	☼ ☼ ☆ ☆ ☆
MAGIC	☼ ☆ ☆ ☆ ☆
SMARTS	☆ ☆ ☆ ☆ ☆
LOOT	☼ ☼ ☆ ☆ ☆
DANGER	☼ ☼ ☼ ☆ ☆

An undead creature brought back from the grave with magic or alchemy. The zombie is the amateur necromancer's first undead minion, mindless, resilient, and easily replaceable. The zombie fills all sorts of low-level positions, from basic servant to footsoldier. Since zombies have no minds and are composed of dead flesh, they feel no pain or fear and will continue to fight even when lacking a limb or two, with the severed body parts continuing to crawl towards their target. The bite of a zombie is filled with disease, and those who receive a bite may find themselves gradually transforming into an undead monstrosity. Ambient evil magic can lead to the spontaneous appearance of zombies, which are ravenous and aggressive without a necromancer to control them.

Adventurer's Tip: It's best to perform some sort of embalming on the body before performing any rituals to ensure structural longevity and control the smell.

The zombie has become one of fiction's most popular horror creatures, fully breaking into the mainstream in 1968 with George Romero's Night of the Living Dead. *Though modern zombies generally rise from the dead en masse because of some mysterious plague, the original Haitian* zombi *(or* zonbi*) was a servant to a sorcerer, controlled through magic and herbs. Of course, the living dead are popular throughout all folklore, there being something intrinsically horrible about the rotting dead attacking the living.*

Further References

Books

Abrahams, Roger, *African Folktales.*

Afanasy'ev, Alexander, *Russian Fairy Tales.*

Alighieri, Dante, *The Divine Comedy.*

Andersen, Hans Christian, *The Snow Queen, The Little Mermaid,* and others.

Baum, L., Frank, *The Oz* series, and others.

Blatty, William Peter, *The Exorcist.*

Borges, Jorge Luis, *Book of Imaginary Beings.*

Bosma, Sam, *Fantasy Sports* series.

Bruce, Scott (ed.), *The Penguin Book of the Undead.*

Campbell, John Gregorson, *The Gaelic Otherworld: Superstitions of the Highlands and Islands and Witchcraft and Second Sight in the Highlands and Islands of Scotland.*

Carroll, Lewis, *Alice's Adventures in Wonderland,* and others.

Cheng'en, Wu, *Journey to the West.*

Clarke, Susanna, *Jonathan Strange and Mr Norrell,* and others.

Collodi, Carlo, *The Adventures of Pinnochio.*

Dahl, Roald, *James and the Giant Peach, The Witches,* and others.

Davis, F., Hadland, *Myths and Legends of Japan.*

Doyle, Arthur Conan, *The Lost World, The Hound of the Baskervilles,* and others.

Dunsany, Lord, *The King of Elfland's Daughter,* and others.

Ellis, Peter Berresfords, *The Mammoth Book of Celtic Myths and Legends.*

Ferdowsi, *Shahnameh.*

Finney, Jack, *The Body Snatchers.*

Friedlander, Gerald, *Jewish Fairy Tales.*

Gaiman, Neil, *The Sandman* series, and others.

Graves, Robert, *The Greek Myths.*

Grimm, Jacob and Wilhelm Grimm, *Children's and Household Tales.*

Grimm, Jacob, *Teutonic Mythology.*

Haddawy, Husain (ed.), *One Thousand and One Nights.*

Hearn, Lafcadio, *Kwaidan: Stories and Studies of Strange Things.*

Henderson, William, *Folklore of the Northern Counties of England and the Borders.*

Hodgson, William Hope, *The Boats of the "Glen-Carrig,"* and others.

Hoffmann, E.T.A., *The Nutcracker and the Mouse-King,* and others.

Homer. *The Odyssey.*

Howard, Robert E., *Conan the Barbarian* short stories, and others.

Hunt, Robert, *The Drolls, Traditions and Superstitions of Old Cornwall: Popular Romances of the West of England.*

Jansson, Tove, *Moomin* series.

King, Stephen, *It,* and others.

Lang, Andrew, *Fairy Books* series, and others.

Lavers, Chris, *The Natural History of Unicorns.*

Lelang, Charles Godfrey, *The Algonquin Legends of New England.*

Lewis, C.S., *The Chronicles of Narnia, The Screwtape Letters,* and others.

Lovecraft, H.P., *Call of Cthulhu,* and others.

Martin, George R.R., *A Song of Ice and Fire* series.

Matheson, Richard, *I Am Legend,* and others.

Matthews, John and Caitlin Matthews, *The Element Encyclopedia of Magical Creatures: The Ultimate A–Z of Fantastic Beings from Myth and Magic.*

Mignola, Mike, *BPRD* series, *Hellboy* series, and others.

Miyazaki, Hayao, *Nausicaa of the Valley of the Wind,* and others.

Morris, William and Eirikr Magnússon (ed.), *The Völsunga Saga.*

O'Donnell, Elliot, *Scottish Ghost Stories.*

Ovid, *Metamorphoses.*

Ozaki, Yei Theodora, *Japanese Fairy Tales.*

Peterson, Joseph H. (ed.), *The Lesser Key of Solomon.*

Pratchett, Terry, *Discworld* series.

Pullman, Philip, *His Dark Materials* series.

Rowling, J.K., *Harry Potter* series.

Sapkowski, Andrzej, *The Witcher.*

Sax, B., *The Mythical Zoo.*

Shakespeare, William, *A Midsummer Night's Dream,* and others.

Shelley, Mary, *Frankenstein; or, The Modern Prometheus.*

Sîn tēqi-unninni (ed.), *The Epic of Gilgamesh.*

Skeat, Walter W., *Malay Magic: Being an Introduction to the Folklore and Popular Religion of the Malay Peninsula.*

Songling, Pu, *Strange Tales from a Chinese Studio.*

Sophocles, *Oedipus Rex.*

Stein, R.L., *Goosebumps* series.

Stoker, Bram, *Dracula.*

Summers, Montague, *The Werewolf in Lore and Legend.*

Swanton, J., *Source Material for the Social and Ceremonial Life of the Choctaw Indians*

Swire, Oha F., *Skye: The Island and Its Legends.*

Thrum, Thomas G., *Hawaiian Folk Tales.*

Tolkien, J.R.R., *The Hobbit, The Lord of the Rings* series, and others.

Topsell, Edward, *The History of Four-Footed Beasts and Serpents.*

Valmiki, *Ramayana.*

Yeats, William Butter, *Fairy and Folk Tales of the Irish Peasantry.*

Films & Television

Anno, Hideaki, dir. *Neon Genesis Evangelion.* 1995-1996, television series.

Armstrong, Samuel, James Algar, Bill Roberts, Paul Satterfield, Ben Sharpsteen, David D. Hand, Hamilton Luske, Jim Handley, Ford Beebe, T. Hee, Norman Ferguson, and Wilfred Jackson, dir. *Fantasia.* 1940, film.

Barker, Clive, dir. *Hellraiser.* 1987, film.

Benioff, David and D.B. Weiss, creator. *Game of Thrones.* 2011-2019, television series.

Browning, Tod, dir. *Dracula.* 1931, film.

Buck, Chris and Jennifer Lee, dir. *Frozen.* 2013, film.

Clement, Jermaine and Taika Waititi, dir. *What We Do in the Shadows.* 2014, film.

Clements, Ron and John Musker, dir. *Hercules.* 1997, film.

Corman, Roger, dir. *The Little Shop of Horrors.* 1960, film.

Dante, Joe, dir. *Gremlins.* 1984, film.

Davis, Desmond, dir. *Clash of the Titans.* 1981, film.

del Toro, Guillermo, dir. *Pan's Labyrinth.* 2006, film.

Dilworth, John R., creator. *Courage the Cowardly Dog.* 1999-2002, television series.

DiMartino, Michael Dante and Bryan Konietzko, creator. *Avatar: The Last Airbender.* 2005-2008, television series.

Djalil, H. Tjut, dir. *Mystics in Bali*. 1981, film.

Fell, Sam and Chris Butler, dir. *ParaNorman*. 2012, film.

Geronimi, Clyde, dir. *Sleeping Beauty*. 1959, film.

Geronimi, Clyde, Wilfred Jackson, and Hamilton Luske, dir. *Alice in Wonderland*. 1951, film.

Gordon, Stuart, dir. *Dolls*. 1987, film.

Honda, Ishiro, dir. *Godzilla*. 1954, film.

Hosoda, Mamoru, dir. *The Boy and the Beast*. 2015, film.

Lang, Fritz, dir. *Metropolis*. 1927, film.

Lasseter, John, dir. *Toy Story*. 1995, film.

Lau, Ricky, dir. *Mr. Vampire*. 1985, film.

Marquand, Richard, dir. *Star Wars: Episode VI – Return of the Jedi*. 1983, film.

McKean, Dave, dir. *MirrorMask*. 2005, film.

Miyazaki, Hayao, dir. *Castle in the Sky*. 1986, film.

Miyazaki, Hayao, dir. *Howl's Moving Castle*. 2004, film.

Miyazaki, Hayao, dir. *Ponyo*. 2008, film.

Miyazaki, Hayao, dir. *Princess Mononoke*. 1997, film.

Miyazaki, Hayao, dir. *Spirited Away*. 2001, film.

Moran, Martha and Phil Harnage, creator. *Street Sharks*. 1994-1997, television series.

Murch, Walter, dir. *Return to Oz*. 1985, film.

Murnau, F.W., dir. *Nosferatu: A Symphony of Horrors.* 1922, film.

O'Bannon, Dan, dir. *The Return of the Living Dead.* 1985, film.

Oomori, Hidetosho, Hiroyuki Kitakubo, Hiroyuki Kitazume, Katsuhiro Otomo, Koji Morimoto, Mao Lamdo, Takashi Nakamura, and Yasuomi Umetsu, dir. *Robot Carnival.* 1987, film.

Øvredal, André, dir. *Trollhunter.* 2010, film.

Raimi, Sam, dir. *The Evil Dead.* 1981, film.

Romero, George A., dir. *Night of the Living Dead.* 1968, film.

Sanders, Chris and Dean DeBlois, dir. *How to Train Your Dragon.* 2010, film.

Selick, Henry, dir. *The Nightmare Before Christmas.* 1993, film.

Serling, Rod, creator. *The Twilight Zone.* 1959-1964, television series.

Shimizu, Takashi, dir. *The Grudge.* 2004, film.

Takahata, Isao, dir. *Pom Poko.* 1994, film.

Tomino, Yoshiyuki, creator. *Mobile Suit Gundam.* 1979-1980, television series.

Verbinski, Gore, dir. *The Ring.* 2002, film.

Ward, Pendleton, creator. *Adventure Time.* 2010-2018, television series.

Whedon, Joss, creator. *Buffy the Vampire Slayer.* 1997-2003, television series.

Wiene, Robert, dir. *The Cabinet of Dr. Caligari.* 1920, film.

Yeaworth, Irvin, dir. *The Blob.* 1958, film.

Yuasa, Masaaki, dir. *Lu Over the Wall.* 2017, film.

Games

Andrews McMeel Publishing. *Zweihander Grim & Perilous RPG*. 2019, tabletop game.

Andrews McMeel Publishing. *Main Gauche Grim & Perilous Supplement*. 2019, tabletop game.

Atlus. *Shin Megami Tensei* series. 1992, video game.

Bethesda Softworks. *The Elder Scrolls* series. 1994, video game.

Blizzard Entertainment, Inc. *Diablo* series. 1996, video game.

Blizzard Entertainment, Inc. *Warcraft* series. 1994, video game.

Capcom. *Ōkami* series. 2006, video game.

Capcom. *Resident Evil* series. 1996, video game.

Cephalofair Games. *Gloomhaven*. 2017, board game.

FASA. *Shadowrun*. 1989, tabletop game.

Games Workshop. *Warhammer*. 1987, tabletop game.

Konami. *Silent Hill* series. 1999, video game.

Konami. *Yu-Gi-Oh! Trading Card Game*. 1999, card game.

Larian Studios. *Divine Divinity* series. 2002, video game.

Namco Bandai Games. *Dark Souls* series. 2011, video game.

Nintendo. *EarthBound*. 1994, video game.

Nintendo. *Mario* series. 1981, video game.

Nintendo. *The Legend of Zelda* series. 1986, video game.

Paizo Publishing. *Pathfinder Roleplaying Game*. 2009, tabletop game.

Riot Games. *League of Legends*. 2009, video game.

Sony Computer Entertainment. *Shadow of the Colossus*. 2005, video game.

Sony Computer Entertainment. *The Last of Us* series. 2013, video game.

Sony Interactive Entertainment. *God of War* series. 2005, video game.

Square Enix. *Dragon Quest* series. 1986, video game.

Square Enix. *Final Fantasy* series. 1987, video game.

The Pokémon Company. *Pokémon* series. 1996, video game and card game.

Ubisoft. *Assassin's Creed* series. 2007, video game.

White Wolf Publishing. *Exalted*. 2001, tabletop game.

White Wolf Publishing. *World of Darkness*. 2004, tabletop game.

Wizards of the Coast. *Dungeons & Dragons*. 1974, tabletop game.

Wizards of the Coast. *Magic: The Gathering*. 1993, card game.

About the Authors

Blanca Martínez de Rituerto is an animator and illustrator living and working in London, England. She has made a comfortable living by animating various advertisements, music videos, show pilots, and films.

She likes to read, read, read, and there's nothing you can do to stop her. Other favorite activities include eating, sleeping, drawing, and gaming of the video and tabletop varieties.

She has too many books and not enough shelves, a trait she may have inherited from her parents.

Joe Sparrow is an illustrator, animator, and comic book artist living and working in London, England. He likes playing videogames with friends, watching literally anything directed by Masaaki Yuasa, and eating food.

In addition to providing character design for television shows such as Cartoon Network's *Adventure Time* and Disney's *Amphibia*, his previous published works include *The Hunter* (Nobrow, 2015), *Homunculus* (ShortBox, 2018), and the *Law Under Love* tarot deck.

He really wants to make a videogame at some point in the next few years.

From the Sketchbook